Everything
I Know
about Dating
I Learned in

Business School

Cover Design by Heather McDonald

Printed in the United States

First Edition

TCB-Cafe Publishing
PO Box 471706
San Francisco, California 94147
USA

ISBN 0-9674898-1-4

Library of Congress Card Catalog Number 2001116179

Everything I Know about Dating
I Learned in
Business School

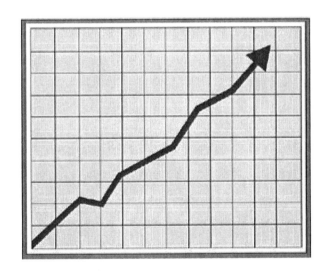

To Stephanie, Sancha, and Randy, who proved that you don't need
an advanced degree to have a great idea, just a good bottle of wine.

Contents

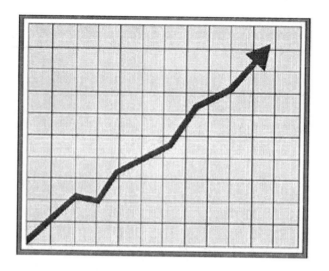

INTRODUCTION

W hat does it take to succeed in today's dating world? One thing is certain, society is constantly changing, and the rules constantly change with it. When once reliance upon a parent, elder or clergyman was enough to guarantee the acquisition of a mate, now individuals are literally on their own. From the days of chaperones and dowries have emerged the nights of uncertainty and personal endurance. The only institutions that are changing as rapidly as society are businesses. In the business world, the rules are simple: Adapt, Profit, Survive.

To succeed in the dating world requires a new approach, an approach based on principles that have guided successful businesses for decades. These principles can be learned from years of experience and hard work, or found in the classes of some of the top business schools. Business schools are perfect microcosms of both the business and dating worlds. Entrance is not guaranteed, and success is far from assured.

On the one hand, hundreds of students simultaneously compete and team with one another to grow, learn, survive, and thrive. Ordinary people from all walks of life with above average grades and high aspirations , they work 20 hour days to achieve good grades, find worthwhile internships, master the basic concepts of profitable free enterprise, and make long-lasting connections that will assistance them in future endeavors.

On the other hand, these same students find themselves to be mature adults, flowing with dynamic energies and at the peak of their sexual prowess, corralled for hours at a time with others of the same type and with the same drives. Tensions build and peak, as not only battles for dominance and control are played out, but also the desire to establish relationships that go far beyond the platonic. In addition to learning the perspective of a Chairman of the Board, business school students are also learning "Who is good date material, where do they sit, and what are my chances?"

Yin and yang in constant turmoil, there is no better place to learn the real secrets of successful dating.

What Do You Want?

Would you like to become more successful in love? Would you like to feel confident that you will actually meet the type of person you desire? Do you want to present yourself so they find you attractive and sexy? Or to know when things are going well, and when it is time to turn up the heat?

What about money? Do you have any idea when you've gone too far and spent too much energy on a relationship, or not enough? Finally, do you want to be so satisfied with your love life that you essentially become a dating mogul?

If you answered "yes" to any of these questions, the first rule of business is to understand the following:

The difference between a merger and an acquisition

In a business merger, two companies come together to share assets, strengths, weaknesses, and resources in order to reach a mutually agreed upon common goal. They work together, plan together, play together, and eat lunch together.

In a business acquisition, one company takes over another company in order to use their assets, strengths, and resources to reach its own self-satisfying goals. In other words, it eats their lunch alone.

Relationships are similar to businesses. Two people can come together with the potential to form a happy merger, or they can consider each other as targets for acquisition. The choices are clear. They can meet on common ground, or on the field of combat.

Unfortunately, combat is common when you operate without the benefit of tried-and-true dating guidelines. These guidelines, as with mergers and acquisitions, come directly from the world of business and commerce [with a dash of insight from the village elders], and are as equally applicable to your love life. They include practices such as product packaging, positioning, and advertising, as well as finance, negotiation, and promotion. Each is required to create and manage a successful business, and each is what you need to use to successfully manage dating. Using these concepts you actually can become a Dating Mogul, if that is your desire. You can have it all - dates on Wednesday, Thursday, Friday, Saturday, and believe or not, even on Monday. You can have it all because unlike your competition, you now the rules of the game. You know the bottom line. You know how to get there. You know the basics.

Getting Down to the Basics

Have you ever read an article in which a wealthy entrepreneur from Slurfenburg says, "Gee, I just sort of kicked my car one day and the next thing I know I'm running this fantastic business"? Do we think this ability to succeed without effort is real? Not particularly. If it were then the entire planet would be vacationing in Fiji right now. Success does not simply happen on its own or by luck, it happens because one way or another people figure out how to take care of "the basics."

You've heard of "the basics." The basics are what coaches talk about when they blow an easy game, or a CEO emphasizes as part of the new plan when quarterly earnings have been missed and their ass is on the line. They've got to get back to "the basics." Why get back to basics, we ask, when you should never forget them. The basics are true because they have one thing in common - they are the foundation for success.

The same bottom line is true in dating. One day you're doing alright, whistling as you walk, singing in the rain, kissing and not telling, and the next you can't even get a returned telephone call. Why? You forgot "the basics." Fortunately, dating basics are very simple. They are essentially the answers to the following questions:

- Who is out there?
- What do they want?
- How can you reach them?
- What do you have that gives you an advantage over the competition?
- How should you package yourself?
- How do you pay for your efforts?
- How do you avoid [or win] disputes?
- How do you deal with money?
- Who do you go to for help?

When you ask these questions and supply answers by using the 'basic', easy-to-understand, and easy-to-use practices outlined in this book, you will become a dating mogul.

You may be under the false assumption that to become a dating mogul all you need to know is how to be a good salesperson. A few good lines here and there and you can close the deal. Our advise is to forget the hard-sell. Unless you really are a salesperson by profession it doesn't work, and even then, not as well as you think. What does work is to think of yourself as an entrepreneur, and your business is You, Ltd. You are a dating enterprise. As part of your strategic plan, you are going to take your firm public, gain market share, create attractive new product features, satisfy suppliers, increase customer loyalty, and expand your portfolio. You will penetrate new niches, make new friends, and really enjoy your life. These objectives are all within your reach. Everything we know about dating and learned in business school is at your disposal.

What Do I Need to Pay?

Keep in mind that though we actually paid for graduate business school, you can reap the unexpected rewards of our education, both in-class and extracurricular. Not only can you learn the basics of dating and commerce, you can do so at approximately .024% of the cost we paid. Plus, you'll save two years of study.

So take what we know and be successful. Remember the basics. Don't forget that even with insider information, there are things that you need to do because dating success doesn't just happen.

You want to succeed in dating? Don't waste another minute. Let's get started.

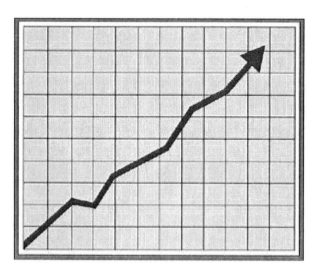

MARKET RESEARCH

"What is research but a blind date with knowledge."
- William Henry

In business as in dating, the key to success is in knowing your market. To create a product that people will buy you have to know what they want or will accept. To sell a product so people can buy it you have to know where they are, and how to reach them. The same is true in dating.

If you look at yourself as a product then proper research can help you define the key elements of your market. This means getting the answers to the three W's: Who's out there, Where to find them, and What do they want?

These are very important questions. They must be answered before you can look at your competitive advantages. They must be answered before you can begin your packaging and positioning. Finally, they must be answered before you can begin creating the kick-ass marketing campaign that leaves potential lovers groveling at your feet.

In the end, isn't that what you want?

What is market research and why do you need it?

Market research can be thought of as the application of scientific method to the solution of marketing problems. It involves studying people as buyers, sellers, and consumers, examining their attitudes, preferences, habits, and purchasing power. Market research is also concerned with the channels of distribution, with promotion and pricing, and with the design of the products and services to be marketed.

All businesses require accurate and timely information to be successful. Whether your company is large or small, the right amount of financing, equipment, materials, talent, and experience alone are not enough to succeed without a constant flow of the right business information. All successful business owners must know their markets, competitors, customer wants and needs, and "what it takes to be competitive." It is not enough to know the answers to what, where, when, and how questions about our businesses. We also need to know why people buy our products and services.

The first step in doing market research is to decide what you really need to find out. Do you need to obtain a general feel for how key target buyers think about your product category and its various types of items, brands, and buying occasions? If so, interviewing groups of target buyers in focus groups may be the way to go, even though

1

this type of research indicates only directional trends and may not be statistically reliable. Or is the confirmation of general trends in your industry sufficient? In that case, reading information from outside information services, industry trade associations, and industry experts may be all that you need to do.

Every business school student is familiar with the Coca-Cola market research story. It is a textbook case of doing the wrong things for the right reasons because of the wrong information. Fortune 500 company Coca-Cola is a classic example of the embarrassing results of shoddy market research. Northwestern University business school professor Philip Kotler writes in Marketing Management, "Coke knows that we put 3.2 ice cubes in a glass, see 69 of its commercials every year, and prefer cans to pop out of vending machines at a temperature of 35 degrees." Still, Coke's research went down the wrong road in a big way.

In the 1980's Coke decided to expand their product line by updating their flagship beverage product, Coke. The replacement was called, in a brilliant stroke of marketing genius, "New Coke." The catchy name alone should have given the Coca-Cola execs some indication that things were a little screwy, but unfortunately they were probably the ones who came up with it.

The impetus for New Coke was what were euphemistically called the Cola Wars. Pepsi vs Coke, Coke vs Pepsi, every other beverage pretending like they mattered (kind of like the American political system). In these Wars all manner of dirty tricks were employed, from witty jingles - Get the Real Thing, Catch the Wave, to Olympic sponsorships, to fancy commercials featuring Michael Jackson, to setting Michael Jackson's hair on fire while shooting the commercials. It was indeed an ugly, desperate time.

Coke realized this and knew it was time to go for broke. However, being conservative businessmen with fiduciary responsibilities (see, CYA), they would not act without some statistical assurance that what they were doing was right. What they needed was market research, the best that money could buy.

To this day no one is really sure what kind of market research was performed by Coca-Cola. Some say they played spin the bottle, others think they pulled it out of their children's diapers. There are even those who mention a fairy godmother in the Coke bottling plants. The best guess we can come up with, though, is that it was the equivalent of a dog sticking their head up your skirt and declaring, "This ain't no dog."

Whatever method they used, it was convincing enough to decide to invest millions of dollars and the future of a multi-national, multi-billion dollar company. Based on their market research Coca-cola was convinced that New Coke was better tasting, more appealing, and would knock the competition off the charts.

The opposite came close to happening. The reality was that many customers liked the somewhat industrial taste of "old" Coke, and when they wanted a Coke experience this is exactly what they anticipated. It didn't matter how much better tasting the upgrade was. In truth, the new product could have been gold-lined, spewed the Fountain of Youth, and given drinkers thirty-five minute orgasms. They did not care. The loyal customers wanted their old Coke, they wanted it now, and were willing to go on national television moaning pitifully about the injustice of it all.

This unexpected turn of events not only scared the crap out of the Coca-cola execs, but freaked the hell out of Pepsi as well. The Cola Wars were mutually declared finished, basically due to the shear bizarreness of the situation.

Needless to say, "old" Coke was continued, "New Coke" was a joke, and a few heads rolled at the Coca-Cola corporate headquarters. Some sly MBA's and journalists still think, however, that this product launch was all part of a crafty Grand Plan, and that New Coke was meant to fail in order to promote old Coke. If you believe that, talk to us about the land we have in the desert, over near Area 51.

Let this be a lesson. Just because you say you're doing market research doesn't mean you're doing it right. Don't go out doing it looking for exactly the answers that you want to hear. Don't get New Coked-up.

The essence of market research is objectivity. You can't decide what you're going to find then figure out how to find it. True, you may have a hypothesis that you want to test, or a product idea that you want to trial, but don't seek to confirm what you already know. If you are so sure that a product will sell that you will risk putting all of your bets on it, then bet away! You've got a 50/50 chance, which is better than Vegas odds. For example, think about your "Ex". Sometimes you always knew how they would react to a certain situation. It happened time and time again, and when you mentioned this fact they would get mad and say you were wrong and full of cow manure. But unfailingly they had the same reaction over and over. In this case do you need market research? No! The reason is you've already done the market research through observation. You've watched what they did and drawn your conclusions. You subsequently used those conclusions to predict their future actions.

This is the level of certainty that you want to achieve in your dating market research. You want to observe, draw conclusions, put them to the test, check the responses, and when you are sure of the results, exploit them until you can no longer stand the intensity of the experience.

Here are some conclusions that we have drawn from our dating market research, and ways they have been applied:

Sample Dating Market Research: Observations & Applications

•Observation: Women like peach-flavored ice cream
•Application: Hang out at Ben & Jerry's and Baskin-Robbins on a Friday night looking for ice-cream jones-ing women

•Observation: Men are either too lazy, too nice, too aggressive, or total jerks
•Application: Talk to their mothers

•Observation: San Francisco is full of single, eligible, attractive women
•Application: Move immediately to San Francisco

•Observation: Alaska is full of single, eligible, breathing men
•Application: Talk about vacationing in Alaska, chicken out because of the cold, find out where Alaskans vacation and go there instead.

•Observation: Everyone wants to pet the cute doggy
•Application: Get a gig as a professional dog walker, but only walk them on Saturday afternoons and on Thursday at lunch hour. Tie them up outside of Starbucks and wait for prey to take the bait.

•Observation: In social settings, single males and females travel in Zebra-like herds for camouflage
•Application: Like a lion[ess] during the hunt, you must cut off an individual from the herd and corner them using wile and cunning

•Observation: People like dates who will listen to them
•Application: Ask a question every 120 seconds, wait 25 seconds, say "yeah, yeah", wait 17.8 seconds, say "uh-huh". Repeat for fifteen minutes to an hour. Keep eyes on subject. Try as much as humanly possible [for guys] not to check out other prospects. Don't fall asleep. End the conversation with, "It was great talking with you, we should get together sometime and do something." (subsequently losing telephone number is an unnecessary embellishment on the technique)

•Observation: Men lose women's telephone numbers before they get home 53% of the time, when they get home 75% of the time, and after three days 95% of the time.
•Application: Carry a tattoo gun and a branding iron

•Observation: Women who like the music of Joni Mitchell are really, really spooky (Stevie Nicks also works)
•Application: Run, don't walk, to the exit! If she's wearing a lace blouse or dress, scream as if your life depended on it.

•Observation: Size really does matter
•Application: Various

Well known methods of market research

There are many tried and true methods for performing market research. The average American is familiar with them in one way or another, usually because they've participated in them while walking down the street or trying to eat dinner. The ones that we will cover in this chapter include the following:

- Polls
- Surveys
- One-on-one interviews
- Focus groups
- Syndicated research

Each of these methods has their strengths and weaknesses, particularly from a dating perspective. To simplify them for you, we've provided a brief summary of each, along with our opinion on how to use them.

POLLS

What the experts say:

> Definition: a questioning or canvassing of persons selected at random or by quota to obtain information or opinions to be analyzed.

> A useful and simple to implement method of ascertaining a large population's opinion on 1-2 topics. Generally confined to one question, with one to four pre-written answers from which to choose.

What we say:

Polls are for very lazy people. You ask a few simple questions, like who would you vote for President, or which supermodel looks better in a topless bikini, or do you find your cat sexy. People pick one option, or answer yes or no. That's it. No detail, no insight. Just very broad generalizations, with unscientific unverifiable conclusions like those you find among women in New York ("Men are assholes"), women in Los Angeles ("Men are snakes"), and women in Wyoming ("Men need to bathe").

On the other hand, unscientific conclusions are perfect for media and political polls, which is why they are everywhere during an election year.

Despite this weakness, polls can be extremely useful for dating in a few special circumstances, if you have the nerve to employ them. For example, if you went up to every person that looked liked a potential date, you could ask them two of the following questions (any more and it's a survey):

"Are you single"
"Do you find me attractive?"
"How attractive (pick one)? - A Little bit, Kind of, Sort of, Very, Mucho"
"Would you ever consider going out with me?"
"Is money more important to you or looks?"
"Is personality more important or money?"
"Which is more important, sex or food?"

Of course, keep in mind that you need to announce that you're taking a poll. Otherwise it just sounds like you're trying out pick-up lines.

SURVEYS

What the experts say:

> Surveys provide quantitative information. Quantitative research is numerically oriented, requires significant attention to the measurement of market phenomena, and often involves statistical analysis. For example, when a restaurant asks its customers to rate different aspects of its service on a scale from 1 (good) to 10 (poor), this provides quantitative information that may be analyzed statistically.

What we say:

Survey's are good in that they give you somewhat definitive answers to many questions, and you can put together a pretty good picture of your market. You can add the answers and come up with totals, percentages, ratios, and all kinds of great stuff that look really good on charts. Plus you can get a good feel for what the majority likes and dislikes. But only if you ask the right questions. The legendary Cosmopolitan survey is a good example. This survey, which receives national press coverage, once came up with a very interesting statistical conclusion:

> "Women over 35 in New York City are more likely to be eaten alive by a shark than to eventually get married"

When this conclusion was published, women over 35 around the country simultaneously reached for the Valium and Vodka, and their mothers reached for the telephone to see if their best friend's recently divorced son was still available.

How do you draw the comparison between marriage and shark attacks? (Married people could probably answer that one without even skipping a beat) Maybe the survey went something like this:

#1 - Sex (M/F)
#2 - How old are you?
#3 - Are you married? (Y/N)

#4 - Are you going to get married? (Y/N)
#5 - Are you going to be eaten by a shark? (Y/N)

As you can see, as with all market research you have to be very careful about how you phrase the question.

In all fairness to Cosmopolitan, they probably looked at the incidence of women who had married after reaching the decrepit age of 35, and the incidence of women being eaten by sharks, and decided that sharks had the edge. What we don't know is if they also compared it to other phenomena like lightening strikes, meteor impacts, ice falling from airplanes, whirlpool drowning, Sasquatch kidnapping, Alien lovefests, and men not losing your telephone number before they call the first time.

ONE-ON-ONE INTERVIEWS

What the experts say:

> The most expensive form of market research, one-on-one interviews allow you to define individual traits, thoughts, preferences, and reactions of your target market at profound level of detail. Due to the time required for each interview, as well as the need to identify and recruit interviewees, one-one interviews, though valuable, consume a great deal of time and energy.

> Additionally, the small sample size may result in false data that is not statistically significant, essentially creating an untrue profile of your target market, and a subsequent waste of your marketing and business resources.

What we say:

This is what happens during most first and second dates, and we know how effective they are. If it doesn't work out then you feel like you've wasted your time, or like something's wrong with you. On the other hand, it does give you first-hand knowledge of the issues. Unfortunately, the information is very biased based on your own perceptions, plus the fact that the interviewee may not have been entirely honest in their responses.

Come on, who actually believes it when they say, "It's not you, it's me"?

FOCUS GROUPS

What the experts say:

> Focus groups are a somewhat informal technique that can help you assess user needs and feelings both before interface design and long

after implementation. In a focus group, you bring together from six to nine users to discuss issues and concerns about the features of a user interface. The group typically lasts about two hours and is run by a moderator who maintains the group's focus.

Focus groups often bring out users' spontaneous reactions and ideas and let you observe some group dynamics and organizational issues. You can also ask people to discuss how they perform activities that span many days or weeks: something that is expensive to observe directly. However, they can only assess what customers say they do and not the way customers actually operate the product. Since there are often major differences between what people say and what they do, direct observation of one user at a time always needs to be done to supplement focus groups.

What we say:

This is the way to go. Something close to objectivity, with the benefits of multiple perspectives. People feel more comfortable answering questions in a group setting, no matter how dumb they sound. After about fifteen minutes they're telling you how they feel on a wide variety of subjects. When someone says, "I prefer blondes", five others chime in with, "Yeah, because you get to ask them if it's real!" Now you're starting to understand your market.

Focus groups are great because all you need is more than three of the test subjects and you can begin. Location is unimportant. Bar, home, work, the gym, each is a usable focus group venue. If they answer the apparently innocent first question, "What do you like in a date?", then you're in.

On the other hand, be careful, because focus groups can mislead you if you don't probe deeply enough. The following focus group discussion is a good example:

> **Focus Group Member A:** All the men around here are either gay, or don't have any social skills
>
> **Focus Group Member B**: Yeah!
>
> **Focus Group Member C**: That's right!
>
> **Us**: Why do you say that, they can't all be gay or socially inept
>
> **Focus Group Member A:** They are, they're not interested in us, just in working out or their computers
>
> **Focus Group Member B:** Losers!
>
> **Focus Group Member C**: That's right!
>
> **Us**: So no men have asked you out recently?

Focus Group Member A: Only guys who think that their stock options are going to impress me

Focus Group Member B: Yeah, or they're gay

Us: A gay man asked you out? How do you know he's gay?

Focus Group Member B: Because he hasn't kissed me

Focus Group Member A: He hasn't kissed you, he's gay alright!

Us: So you're just friends then, what's the big deal? You thought it was going to be more?

Focus Group Member B: Maybe. He still sends me flowers after four months. He's a sweetie

Us: He sent flowers after four months?

Focus Group Member B: Yeah. Actually now that I think about it, he did try to kiss me once

Us: Really, how do you know?

Focus Group Member B: A woman knows these things. He did 'the lean.'

Focus Group Member C: Oh yeah, 'the lean!'

Us: So did you kiss him?

Focus Group Member B: Nope. I stopped him by just looking straight ahead. I had some big deliverables due at work, and didn't want to be distracted.

Us: And he never tried to kiss you again?

Focus Group Member B: Not yet

Us: And you think that he's gay?

Focus Group Member B: ...maybe, anyway, I know that I can have him if I want him

Focus Group Member C: Give him to me.

Focus Group Member B: Well, I'm not interested him in that way anymore

As you can see, market research of any type is only as good you make it. As they say, "there are statistics, damn statistics, and lies."

What the experts say:

> Syndicated research is often performed by a research firm or analyst group without a specific request by a client. The firm is known as an industry expert, and the creation of publication of research reports providers a the reader in-depth information that they normally may not be able to afford with customized or sponsored research. This research is generally available to any party or competitor that can afford the purchase price.

> Syndicated research studies are a cost-effective tool for examining trends, reading the findings and conclusions of industry experts, and understanding the direction of the industry. Well known providers of syndicated research studies include Gallup, Nielsen, the Gartner Group, the Yankee Group, and Forrester Research.

What we say:

Read a magazine, it's much cheaper, and you'll get the same results.

Where do you conduct market research?

The best places to conduct market research are where you are likely to find your target market. Bars are a good example. Most people in bars are conducting market research of one kind or another. Often it's very basic, consisting of demographic information such as, "How many hot babes are here?", or, "Do any of these guys have jobs?" Market research at bars, when they don't culminate in an actual "sale", generates basic yet essential information.

Good dating market research should take place everywhere you go, with everyone you know and meet, all the time. To be the dating mogul that you are destined to become means that you have to keep your finger on the pulse of the market. Remember, "Keep your finger on it."

Take the old stand-by, the wedding reception. Everyone knows that weddings are made for dating market research. As soon as you step through the door, helpful "strategic partners" are pointing out other available parties, along with vital statistics like, "She just broke up with her boyfriend, very nice but kind of a freak," and, "I've seen him at five wedding this year, and he's always drinking the champagne out of women's shoes." Weddings are a hotbed of future aspirations, broken dreams, and opportunities to hook up.

Movies are another good example. What do we mean when we say, "chick flick" or "guy film"? Ordinary people say it to signify that if you're not in the group described then you won't be interested in the film except as a way to please your date. The business school dating guru knows that this glass is half-full, not half-empty. Movies are actually networking and market research opportunities combined. Look at the line for refreshments. Ask yourself the following questions: Who's standing in line and buying Junior Mints? How much butter are they requesting on their popcorn, and does it really correlate to weight, or more to a sexually frustrated look in their eyes? Is the person alone, or with platonic friends? Can you find a way to get in line behind them and start a conversation? Can you find out where they're sitting so you can leave the movie after them and suggest what a great piece of art the film was, and would they like to get a drink to discuss it further? Can you remember everyone's faces in case you see them again at the grocery? Yes, indeed, now you see the possibilities.

Two cardinal rules of market research are to always ask questions, and always be observant. If you want to know where you might meet dates, the best way to find out is to ask those who have dates, significant others, or spouses where they met. Don't be afraid to ask all of them this simple question: "Where did you meet?" The answers you get could be your ticket to romance.

Sound a little too simple? It isn't. The following is a set of real answers to that question:

- At school
- At a friend's house
- At the country-western bar on "west coast swing" night
- At a swing dance class
- Jogging
- At a bar
- At a wine tasting course
- We were part of the same group of friends
- At a photography class
- At work
- On the bus stop
- At my apartment (a friend of my roommates)
- At a weekend long wedding party
- In the political group to which I belong
- At a party

Getting the picture? You can meet people anywhere, you just have to be in close proximity for a certain length of time (in some cities, "at the bus stop" is a very long length of time). In some ways the answer to meeting people is simply that of getting out of the house and pursuing your own interests. The problem is when you don't have any interests. That's when you really need to follow someone else's lead.

But asking the question, "where did you meet?" is only half the solution.

You have to ask the next question, the more important one, which tells how they actually became interested in each other. That's where the real kernels of wisdom come through:

"Were you interested in each other right away?"

- At school
- "No, not until about three months into the semester. We both were working on the same assignment and were studying with a mutual friend in the class. They left early, and we started talking. After that we were comfortable calling each other up and going out, and one thing led to another."
- At a friend's house
- "[The friend] had some people over to watch the game, and instead of watching the game we were joking about the food and lack of enough beer. Since everyone was glued to the set, we saw we had the same sense of humor."
- At the country-western bar on "west coast swing" night
- "You go often enough you get to dance with everyone, because it's the "west coast swing." I'm not really the best looking person at the bar, but I am a lot of fun to dance with, and so I ended up dancing with a lot of people. Next thing I know I've got people asking if I wanted to go out later. That started happening about after five weeks. I went to the bar to dance twice a week. Eventually I had to decide on one person, though. I don't know when they decided I was the one, probably earlier than that."
- At a swing dance class
- "Unless you go with a partner, swing dance classes are basically a respectable version of a singles bar. Everyone there wants to meet someone. I'm just glad that [they] took me serious when I asked [them] if they wanted to practice outside of class. He said 'yes,' so I'd have to say that he was interested."
- Jogging
- "You run the same routes every day at the same time and you end up seeing the same people. If they run about your speed you sometimes run together, and then you start talking about what you do, where you go for fun, what you like to eat. We started that way, and it was like we had a date every morning. But you know, a lot of people jog together without having any romantic feelings, so you've got to be careful. But since we both did start warming up to each other, it wasn't very long before we were hanging out during the evening and the morning, or vice versa. I think it was about two weeks from our first run together."
- At a bar
- "Yeah, you know that you're really not going to meet the love of your life in a bar, but you do meet a lot of people, or at least see a lot people. We were both there with our friends, and the two groups starting talking after one of the guys in our group knew one of the guys in the other group. Next thing you know we're all kind of

mingling. Since it was a bar, you sort of assume that if you're talking to someone that's your type for long enough they're going to know that you're interested. So I guess we were interested in each other right away."

- At a wine tasting course

- "Same interests, same ability to pay for the course, same relaxed feeling after a few tasting glasses and hors d'oeuvres. We were definitely interested in each other after the second course."

- We were part of the same group of friends

- "I think it took about five months before I even asked her out, and that's five months after she broke up with her boyfriend. You know how it is, you find them attractive but they're in a relationship. Then they're not, but is it too soon to make a move, or will they not be interested because we're in the same group of friends. You never know. But she gave me a chance... or maybe she thinks that I gave her a chance."

- At a photography class

- "I think that he was flattered when I asked if he wanted to model for me."

- At work

- "I was physically attracted immediately, but he says he thought I was cute but didn't think about me in that way until we had worked together for a while. Then I guess I became "really cute", something to do with looking better over time. You know, wearing them down. But that's cool, because I know he's into me, and not just how I look. It's touchy though, you don't want anyone at work to know, especially if it goes bad. But the weird part is that there are office romances all over the place, even people who claim they don't do it have had them. Because it makes sense. Who do you spend most of your time with? Who's going to know what you're like eight to ten hours a day? I say, 'always keep your options open.'"

- On the bus stop

- "We spent ten to thirty minutes a day together waiting for the bus, after a while you're gonna' notice a person. I liked what I saw, and one day I just made a comment about the amount of time we wasted standing on the corner. It went from there to sitting together when there were available seats, to having lunch, to seeing a movie, and the rest is history. But I'm glad I didn't just make a move on them the first few times I saw them waiting for the bus. They would've thought I was a creep."

- At my apartment (a friend of my roommates)

- "My roommates know me, and since I'm not a jerk they're not going to say anything about me to turn off this person. Anyway, they had some people over by the place, and we just hit it off. Since they knew where I lived they could stop by to see me or the roommates. It could have been annoying, like a stalker, but I was into it."

- At a weekend long wedding party

- "I knew so many people at this party that went from Friday till the wedding on Sunday, but there were a lot of people there I didn't know, and this guy was one of them. Of course he was a friend of a friend. I thought he was cool on Friday, and really great by Saturday. By Sunday I was in love."

• In the political group to which I belong
- "If I were cynical I'd say that some people work at these organizations just so they can try to pick someone up. Maybe they do. I don't, I believe in the party's platform. And it took me a long time to figure out that [she] was interested in me. When I did I felt like an idiot. Fortunately, she was still interested."

• At a party
- "We just lucked out. Most people you meet at parties are good for one, maybe two dates. We just kept going out until we were married."

A common theme in each of the responses is also a basic business tenet: No risk, no reward. Out of all of your market research, we are sure you will find that the most valuable, and usable, piece of information.

Don't forget: No risk, no reward. Or conversely, the higher the risk, the higher reward required.

A Sample Practice-Survey

Which do you consider sexier?
• Asparagus
• Cherries
• Walnuts
• Peaches

Which is more romantic?
• Sunrise
• Sunset
• Full Moon
• High Noon

Which is more fun to eat?
• A ripe, juicy Plum
• A ripe, juicy Pomegranate
• A ripe, juicy Nectarine
• A ripe, juicy Date

Which is more fun to peel?
- Apples
- Bananas
- Grapes
- A Trojan

Do you mostly date people:
- Exactly your age
- Less than five years older
- Less than five years younger
- More than five years older
- More than five years younger
- Older than Sin
- Younger than Legal

When you meet someone new, what part of their face do you look at first?
- Their mouth
- Their eyes
- Their nose
- Their hair
- Their nose hair

Of the ones listed below, which part of the body do you find sexiest?
- The Hands
- The Legs
- The Chest
- The "Derriere"
- The Tongue

To which detail do you pay the most attention to on a first date?
- Clothing
- Job
- Crotch

Which is your dream home?
- Old Victorian fixer-upper
- Spanish style Hacienda
- White picket fence cottage
- Penthouse condo with a view
- Suburban ranch or bungalow
- Castle in the Alps
- Cave in the Himalayas
- Barbie's pad

Which animal describes your sexual appetite?
- Camel
- Panda
- Horse
- Rabbit
- Dog
- The legendary horse-sized rabbit-dog

Which is least necessary in a successful date?
- Personality
- Creativity
- Integrity
- Sanity

It looks like you've got the hang of it. Don't just go out there blindly swinging and hoping to connect. Do your research first.

Now you are ready to seek the answers to the Really Big Questions, the Three W's.

- Who's out There?
- Where to Find Them?
- What do They Want

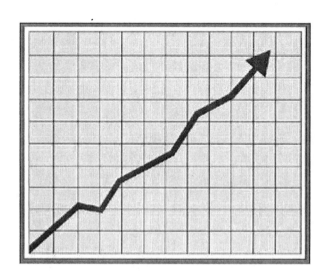

COMPETITIVE ADVANTAGE
: "Using What You've Got"

"Concentrate your strengths against your competitor's relative weaknesses"
- Bruce Henderson

In the 18th century, Adam Smith wrote "The Wealth of Nations", in which he claimed that every country has a unique competitive advantage, one which they should exploit in their trade with other nations. This advantage could be in wheat, oil, cotton, wood, marijuana, pokemon, or other unique services or products (see, Thailand). The point is that if Country U specialize in them then Country U will enjoy a favorable trade balance, since everyone wants what U has and no one else can beat U in their area of expertise.

Though trade is no longer that simple (look at who leads the world in automobiles, televisions, and hyped-up cartoons), the fact is that this philosophy is the very basis of our free market system. If everyone concentrates on doing what they do best, the free market will enjoy the fruits of better products, flowing trade, profitability, lasting happiness, nirvana, and multiple orgasms (sounds promising doesn't it?).

So you want to get in on this "positive balance of trade" thing? First, you must define your competitive advantage. To find your competitive advantage in the free market of the dating world you must ask yourself, "What distinctive competence do I have that gives me a real advantage over my competition?" or "What can I do that no one else does?"

- Argue with my mother? (no)
- Piss-off my ex? (no)
- Chug three beers in sixty seconds? (impressive, but no).

It doesn't really matter at this point what your C.A. happens to be, you're just trying to get to the level where you can be honest with yourself. Honesty is important, at least with yourself. You are, however, allowed to embellish the facts with other people, that's a normal part of Advertising.

Your distinctive competence can be anything, or many things, and it doesn't have to be confined to tangible goods. For example, you may be the only person you know who appreciates the teenage boy band Menudo, the source of Ricki Martin. Assuming that in your neighborhood Menudo-lovers aren't ridiculed and stoned on sight, then one of your competencies is that you "are the person who truly appreciates Menudo."

How does something as off the wall, kind of weird, and kind of "Eighties" as liking Menudo translate into a positive impact on your dating life? As strange as it sounds, it makes a positive impact because it makes you different. In this era, different is good. Unless at this very moment you are actually either still in high school, Amish, living in a war-torn nation where nicknames are reason enough to shoot your neighbor, or from America's Deep, DEEP South, being different equals being attractive.

Of course, being different is a difficult pill to swallow. Most people like to simply follow the crowd. Out of the shear ease of it, they want to be a part of a homogenous group, or at the very least to not stand out. In your current dating circle uniformity may be a standard criteria. Matching colors, matching shirts, matching hair, matching IQ's. But if you, the MBA Dating Machine, are going to succeed then you have to find an aspect of yourself that's unique. If you don't and just follow the movements of the entire dating herd, then you'll become what is known in the business world as a 'commodity'. A harsh fact is that commodities compete primarily based on the lowest price.

Do you really want to be the cheapest date?

What does all this self-assessment mean when you're checking yourself out in the mirror, thinking, "Yeah baby, I'm bad!" Not a lot if you've picked the wrong horse.

Face it, most people have very questionable taste, especially in clothing and fashion. It's a fact of life. You see a man walking down the street in a pair of dotted orange slacks and a tight brown polo shirt over a flopping beer gut, and wonder if he's going to a meeting at the Water Buffalo Camouflage Club. That very same day, you run into a woman wearing the latest fashion trend, hand-sewn pants made of naturally-recycled diapers, and people stare slack-jawed as she walks down the street. Construction workers, trying hard to live up to their well-earned reputation for embarrassing women, are left speechless, as she has beat them to the punch.

Mr. Water Buffalo and Ms. Avant Garde - what do you think you're doing? Why do you dress this way? What target market are you trying to capture? Is market share really worth going through this?

These kinds of misguided attempts to play up, or even create, non-existent fashion strengths are the sad consequences of faulty self-analysis. This error is easily recognized when other people start mumbling within earshot, "What the heck were they thinking?", followed by puzzled lingering looks and cynical glances. Unfortunately, these periods of competitively disadvantageous behavior aren't reserved to the terminally clueless. Everyone has them, especially when trying to decide which personal weaknesses to hide and which strengths to emphasize. Try as we might, for some reason we're always getting it backwards. In our bones we just know that we look hot in that green suede vest and red plaid shorts.

Though high school counselors don't advise it, nor do the talk shows that most people turn to for adult therapy, have you ever taken a good, hard, objective look at yourself? Have you ever tried to understood what makes you great and special, what makes you kind of plain and annoying, and what makes you just like other people? Then, having done this, have you compared yourself in the same way to your dating competition? Or, are you operating completely on gut-feeling, subscribing to the "I'm OK the way I am, Take it or Leave it" philosophy? The self-same philosophy which apparently relies on a major celestial event in order for the perfect date to find you.

This 'good, hard, objective look at yourself' is called identifying your competitive advantage. Remember, a competitive advantage is an area in which you not only have distinct and identifiable competence, but which you can actually leverage to gain an advantage over the competition. It is completely relative in terms of environment, situation, market characteristics, target customers, and comprehensibility, yet it's what makes Coke the King of Soft Drinks, McDonald's the Emperor of Fast Food, and Jiffy Lube a pretty darn good place to have your oil changed when you discover that it's almost at zero.

Below is an actual email sent by a young gent in San Francisco, informing a young woman of her competitive situation when she emailed him with a few get-to-know-you questions . . . like "what's your last name?" :

> "I am at a stage in my life where I'm looking seriously and systematically for someone I can share my life with. You seem like a nice person, and I don't mean this as badly as it might sound, but I don't have time for twenty questions by email. I met five girls Saturday night, have already booked a first coffee with three of them, and meet more every time I go dancing . . . and I go dancing at least three times a week. I immediately rule out women who put up too many barriers. I don't do this because I think there's anything wrong with them, nor do I do it because I'm arrogant. I do this simply to economize on time.
>
> I know that dating in this city is difficult and scary for women. But keep in mind it's that way for the guys, too. Most of all, remember that you're competing with thousands of other women who don't insist that the man do all of the work of establishing a connection. And they live closer.
>
> Now, maybe you'll find someone who's so taken by a single dance with you that he's willing to negotiate by email for a chance to trek to your suburban hideout to plead his case. But you might not. And if such a person does exist, and you do happen to cross paths with him --what do you imagine a guy that desperate would have to offer?
>
> > > > -X.X. (name withheld for obvious reasons)"

Close your mouth. You're probably wondering who we're going to roast, him or her. Well he comes later, in another chapter. For now we'll talk about her.

Despite his attitude, this guy knows something about competitive advantage that apparently she doesn't, which is basically that she doesn't have much. As he says, she's in a city full of women, many intelligent, many attractive, and many ready to go out with a superficial self-absorbed fellow like him who probably couldn't get a date in high school but is King of the World now. To him, she has zero attributes that make her stand out from the rest of the women in the bar. She likes to dance. So do a lot of people. She's a lot of fun. So are Cheetos. She's a single woman. "That's my point", he says.

But this genius is not the expert. The MBA Dating Professors are, and this is our advice: "Forget the creep, no woman will be satisfied even if they do land him. He's a pompous windbag. Though it is true that the customer is always right, for him we would have to say, 'Let the Buyer Beware.' Instead of taking what comes out of his mouth as nuggets of wisdom, she should find something else that will move her up the dating food chain, like trying hang-gliding, or fashion modeling."

Hang-gliding or modeling? Can we be serious?

Indeed we are. Everyone cannot be a successful fashion model, but we've got a little secret to share. Most people who say they are models are not. They either A) Want to be models, B) Are trying to be models, or C) Have taken a few photos for the personal hygiene products in the window of the neighborhood pharmacy. That's the extent of 85% of the folks who say that they model. "Look over here everyone, it's Father Joe the Modeling Priest. And here comes Rabbi Sam, check him out striking that pose. Go Rabbi, go Rabbi, go Rabbi!"

Get serious. Models are basically a consensual hallucination, and that works in your favor. Consensual hallucination is the bedrock of Advertising. It's like looking at a rock and slowly convincing everyone that it's "real purdy." With enough effort, a lot of people will eventually agree. Voila, "consensual hallucination," or as some would say, the secret behind modeling.

What is a model anyway but someone who other people think is very cute. Well, your parents think that you are very cute, don't they?

Work on expanding that base.

The fact is that you really don't have to be a Cindy Crawford, Iman, or Tyra Banks to be attractive because you're a model. You just have to "say" that you're a model. That's enough to make your name, profession, and telephone number shine like fluorescent paint in the eyes of the next guy you meet.

"She's a model, she's a model, she's a model," is what he'll tell his room-mates, his drinking buddies, and his boss at work for the next five days. "I met this girl last weekend, and she's a model," is what you want him to put on the hotline, as part of you viral marketing campaign.

Viral marketing works extremely efficiently because you use other people to spread your product message. In this case, once he tells everyone your model status, he'll continually hear back the following positive reinforcement: "Dude, you gonna call that model?" and "Whatever happened with that model?"

Voila, instant competitive advantage.

Now, let's flip this around for the guys. What can a man do to compete in a world full of successful stock brokers, doctors, surfers, massage therapists and professional athletes? The first thing he needs to do is decide what he wants. Does he want a simple date, a sexual partner, or a potential relationship. Critical questions, as each of these objectives requires a different competitive advantage and marketing strategy.

Always Know Your Competitive Advantage

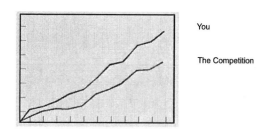

You

The Competition

(For example, if she wants a relationship and he wants a sexual partner, the metrics of achievement change. In this situation, his success becomes known as a "conquest," but if she uses that to reach her goal, he becomes "whipped.")

As described, there many possible competitive advantages.

As a very normal and healthy male with mixed heritage, I grew up with what I now know was a "gift", although I can't say for sure where I got my green eyes. My great-grandfather might have had them, I'm not certain. Either way, I grew up having people stare at my eyes. No big deal, really, until I started dating, then it was "katie bar the door."

More often than not my eyes would be the first thing ladies would comment on, even though I felt my quick wit should be worth some mention too.

After all these years I have finally come to terms with my green eyes; they have always been my ace in the hole, so to speak.

I now have a 16 year old daughter who would kill to have my eyes, even though she has very beautiful brown eyes that turn many a young boy's head. She still doesn't know that she has a "gift" too.

Any feature can really be the one that makes you stand out from the crowd. You just have to be observant.

> Ever since I was 17, people have been telling me what great lips I have. The compliments were nice, but I really didn't pay much attention to them until I was about 25, and had just moved to a new city.
>
> Everything was new, and I had to buy new furniture, some new clothes, stuff like that. I got this old antique mirror at a flea market, and one day I was looking in it, and for some reason I actually noticed my own mouth. I was thinking, "Yeah, I guess it is kind of sexy." So I figured that if everyone liked it I would start emphasizing my assets.
>
> I went out and bought new lipstick. I began pouting my lips like those girls on television. I made sure that when I talked I got close enough for the person to see my lusciousness. But nobody did. No one ever said they liked my lips. It was kind of depressing.
>
> Then one day a friend just came out said to me, "I think you wear too much lipstick."
>
> I was really surprised, because I thought the lipstick would bring out my mouth. It turned out though that I was using too much for me, and it was distracting everyone from their natural appeal. Instead of high-lighting my lips, I was disguising them. Ever since that day I made sure that if I wore lipstick, it worked with me, not against me.

Competitive advantages can work for you if you know how to use them right. Have you ever seen that strange lady with the really long finger nails, the ones that curl around in circles and are painted some color you wouldn't even see in Picasso's crayon box? Why is she growing her nails to such an extreme length? Do you think that it's because she likes not being able to put on her pants like a normal person, or not being able to scratch her nose without giving herself rhinoplasty? No way! She does it because it's her thing, her competitive advantage. It's what makes her stand out from all the people around her.

Take a lesson from her. She understands the concept, but she's got it backwards. What Nail-Lady actually has is a competitive disadvantage. How many dates have you seen her out on, with men or women? Who actually wants to be seen with someone who wasn't unfortunate enough to be born disfigured or hurt in an accident, but purposely makes herself look like an invalid from the Ming Dynasty? Get with the program baby!

Holes in your nose - maybe. Tattoos on your neck - maybe. Long curly freaked-out side-show nails - wrong!

Hit or miss is what you get when you don't use business principals in dating. Sad to say, not all good romances stem from common sense. They need professional help. Everyone thinks they know what you need to attract dates and mates, particularly since it really hasn't changed much over the centuries. Look at the three most common romance-launching product features in human society:

- **Beauty** : Beauty attracts dates. "Great legs" are hot, a "nice smile" is sexy, and a "good body" gets the old hormones popping like Rice Crispies in milk.

- **Money** : Money attracts dates. Being able to afford food and clothing are the starting point, and it just keeps getting better from there.

- **Power** : Power attracts dates. In fact, Power *REALLY* attracts dates. Power is the Trump card of dating .

Face it, you could be a top candidate for the "ET Award - Extraterrestrial of the Year", but if you are also rich and famous then there are thousands of candidates willing to overlook any minor product defects. In time, they'll probably end up finding these traits quite enduring. Just check out Prince Charle's ears, or Shannon Doherty's cubist "Picasso"-eyes. On planet Earth, the rich and powerful have always been able to skip many of the set requirements for dating success.

The people who really understand competitive advantage are athletes. They make great use of what they've got. It may not be brains. It may not be personality. It may not even be real success. But sports figures are prime examples of people who have taken attributes that make them stand out, and turned them into highly attractive biological neon signs subliminally advertising, "Come here. Come here and mate with me many, many times. We will have strong children and great sex. Come... come.... come...."

Of course it's quite natural to find a person attractive who can use their body in ways that make you gasp. Men usually get the vapors watching a woman do splits. Watch their faces closely. "Whoaa, that is the ph-, ph-, phenomenal!!" So much for evolution. Let's examine where it all began.

The first Neanderthal who picked up a twig between fingers and thumb was obviously the most successful down the evolutionary trail. Other cavefolk were probably lined up around the block to get into the bear skins of that advanced specimen. It was unavoidable. We are hard-wired to look for physical prowess. Even if their appearance looks like they'd eat us for dinner in the locker room, if that jock outplays their opponents blindfolded, endorses a clothing line, and builds a castle on a hill in Outer Hackensack, most of us will conveniently ignore their potential lethality. We will actually line up in our Sunday Best to buy a ticket for the dating raffle.

Mike Tyson was a perfect example. What kind of twisted reality did his dates and wives exist in during their first good night kiss? (Was the gold tooth tasty?...oh, let's stop right there. Too much imagination can be a scary thing)

Athletes really do have a true competitive advantage. We all knew girls in high school who would only date jocks, and guys who would only date cheerleaders, and jocks who would only date other jocks. Intelligence and personality did not matter, and it didn't matter if they were either geniuses or morons. For better or worse, high school, and in some cases college, clearly illustrates the sad story of our basic instincts.

A friend tells, "I saw a popular football player once get deliriously happy from playing the role of 'strobe light' at a college party. His talent seemed to be his ability to keep flicking the light switch on and off. Back and forth, on and off, up and down. Now and then he'd get confused. Unfortunately, no one was brave enough to tell him to stop, so we had 'disco boogie-down night' going on for hours. But I've got to tell you, even without the brain cells, that guy did not go home alone."

Television and magazine advertising inflames this freaky situation by making athletes into cultural heros. Who has the willpower to resist a hero? Heros make the very best dating material. Despite what you see on TV and at the movies, studs like Hercules, Superman, Arnold, Bruce, Denzel Washington, Chow Yun Fat, and Xena would never have a problem getting dates any and all days of the year.

Bottom line, being a hero is a damn good competitive advantage. If you can make it happen, more luck to you.

Now that you've got the hang of the competitive advantage concept, let's put it to use. The following is an exercise known as the SWOT Analysis. The SWOT Analysis was originally created by an overpaid East Coast consulting firm in order to impress its underperforming clients. This consulting industry tool became so profitable that everyone started using it, so now business schools across America from Harvard to Hattlebrook make it a required part of a young MBA's education. First-year business students, a particularly impressionable bunch willing to share their new-found knowledge with everyone within ear shot, are known for using the SWOT in practically every new situation they encounter, walking down halls indignantly demanding, "Have you done a SWOT? Why haven't you done a SWOT? I'd have done a SWOT! Let's do a SWOT!!!"

For this reason, we're going to make the SWOT Analysis a part of your dating education.

SWOT stands for Strengths, Weaknesses, Opportunities, and Threats. It is one of the most widely used business tools for companies trying to understand their competitive position in the market, and how best to exploit it. The way SWOT works is simple. Alone, or with a group, you create a chart with four columns across the top - S, W, O, T. Your task is to unbiasedly complete each of these columns with data about yourself. Ask yourself each of these questions:

- "What are my real strengths"
- "What are my real weaknesses?", or "Where am I weak?"
- "Based on the above, and on my environment and life, what are the

opportunities "

- "Based on the above, and on the competitive environment, what are the Threats"

The key to this analysis is complete honesty, with yourself and from others. No fudging, hedging, or polite "No comments." Once completed, the quality of information that a SWOT analysis produces is unbelievable. From this information, useful insights readily emerge, such as how much you should emphasize certain personal features to the customers of the dating market, where you should be looking for cut-throat competition, where you should take advantage of a situation, and what you should forget as delusional.

> Doug is a 29 year old Ph.D. in Architecture. He has traveled extensively, and has lived on three continents. Because of this, and his outgoing nature, Doug has friends and associates around the world, and keeps in close correspondence with most of them. Doug likes a variety of music, and like dancing. More than anything, Doug has no qualms about dancing. In fact, he loves it. Usually when the music starts, he is the first guy to ask women to dance. He knows that often women can't get their dates to dance, or sometimes don't even have a date, and he is more than willing to cut a rug with any forlorn lass.

> Sometimes after dancing, Doug tries to get their telephone number, or set up a date, or start an interesting conversation. Many times, though, they say what a great dancer he is, and then excuse themselves.

Now, let's take a look at Doug's self-described SWOT analysis.

Doug the Dancing Architect
(Our comments in parenthesis)

Strengths	Weaknesses	Opportunities	Threats
Very intelligent (his thesis was titled, "Imaginary numbers... friends or foe?")	Slender (actually, kind of scrawny and soft)	Disco could come back (and for some people it has, for now)	Disco could come back, but not in the place where he lives (making him a pretty good target for other purposes)
Loyal friend (doesn't tell anyone about your many affairs... because he really likes the stories)	Needs new barber (hair style rejected for "Revenge of the Nerds Part 6")	Could meet someone dancing	Could meet no one dancing because they start running away after ten minutes
Great dancer (does the Boogaloo, the Funky Chicken, the Bump, the Slide, Cabbage Patch, and the East Coast Swing)	Glasses and clothing are extremely on the edge...of what he wore in third grade	Could update total look ,-glasses, shirts, pants, hair- to match vibrant personality ("vibrating pants" is more like it)	Could update dress code to the wrong era (what's a "Flapper?")
Worldly yet laid back (lived abroad and discovered he can eat anything and not throw up... smoked some pot once in Rome)	Hasn't been on a successful date in two years (hasn't successfully had sex in four years, which is obvious from the way he can't stop looking at breasts, and the funny way he adjusts his pants upon standing)	Learns to keep his girl friends as friends, in order to get a steady stream of "I know a guy who's single" introductions to their friends (the "sales lead")	May run out of female friends who tolerate his advances (we call that, "burning your bridges")
Quite Clean (except those nails and the snowstorm of dandruff on his head)	Expert in the "gotcha" maneuver. (Alway asks women out within five minutes of their first conversation)	Learns to leverage his intellect and experience (So he will think before he attacks)	He might reproduce

Not a long list, but very revealing. Doug is trying to use the _dancing ritual_ as a way to meet women. Says Doug, "If it works for birds it'll work for me!" Yet, Doug has not worked on the other requirements necessary for success with this practice, such as "personal style" and that little thing we humans call "tact". Though dancing is a strong competitive advantage, it cannot stand alone. Doug has yet to realize this. Instead, he comes off like Bill Murray's version of a Las Vegas lounge lizard, trying to pick up "chicks" and threatening to ask their astrological sign when they stop to catch their breath.

On the other hand, Doug has just barely scratched the surface with his strengths. What is definite is that his greatest weaknesses are self-inflicted, such as trying to date every woman he meets, including his friends. This non-focused, wide-dispersal marketing technique is akin to a telemarketer who calls you during dinner, asking you to change long-distance service, not knowing that you just did last week. Their lack of market research is evident, their timing is poor, and their execution is ill-planned. In sum, you hate them, and wish them an eternity in the 14th Ring of Hell (the one where you can never eat or sleep because the phone is always ringing).

Doug's largest threat is that he is running out of female associates. In addition to the fact that losing friends is never fun, Doug is also eliminating his access to two important areas: Information, and his female friends' female friends. By making himself uninvited for fear of unwanted solicitation, Doug is stifling the flow of competitive information (who's dating who), critical market demographics (where the women hang out), and profitable opportunities (she just broke up with her boyfriend). Without this intelligence, Doug is left to his own devices to refine his product and to locate new target markets. Without these sources Doug's market position is weakened, and he is essentially sinking his own ship.

So what conclusions have we drawn from Doug's SWOT? After thorough study and based on our analysis, we have concluded that Doug's true competitive advantage and possibilities can be described as the following: Loyal, intelligent, slightly-built, mama-dressed, booty-shaking, snake-baking, gun-jumping, creepy-haired, stoner dude. His target market lives in Marrakech.

Competitive Advantage is something that we should all seek to understand about ourselves in the dating market. It leads to less frustration, more efficiency, and enhanced chances of success. The SWOT analysis is just one of several tools that you can use to identify your CA, and it is also one of the simplest and most effective. It's also better than standing in the mirror looking at yourself. Understanding your competitive advantage though, is just the beginning. As we can see from Doug's example, even with a strong and identifiable competitive advantage, if a product is badly packaged and mistakenly positioned, as is Doug's, then satisfactory sales will not result. Effective Packaging and Positioning, therefore, are the next steps in your dating operations.

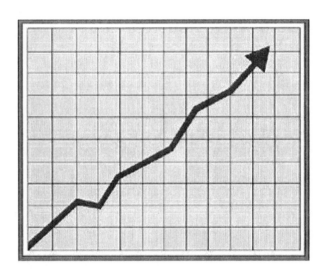

PACKAGING & POSITIONING

"Beware of all enterprises that require new clothes"
- Henry David Thoreau

"The Merit of originality is not novelty, it is sincerity."
- Thomas Carlyle

"I'm not ugly, but my beauty is a total creation"
- Tyra Banks

You understand your market. You know where they are. You know what they want. You want to give it to them. But how should you do it? How will they understand the sweetness that is you? To make the most of what you have to offer, your first action is to segment the potential market.

Market Segmentation

Before moving into product packaging and positioning, you need to figure out a little more about your audience. Who are you trying to target, who are you trying to reach, what common traits do they share? You could always try to go after everyone in the market and see what good fortune comes your way, but you will waste a lot of energy and time on unqualified and undesirable candidates. Your goal is be more focused in your efforts, and this means market segmentation comes first.

Companies have to understand the customer needs that they can satisfy, as well as to whom they belong. No one product can satisfy all of the people all the time in a truly competitive fashion. Therefore the company needs to focus. But there are many variables, and a company has to identify and understand the different preference groups, or segments, of customers and decide which group(s) they should target.

Western consumers are composed of many market segments. They can be divided broadly by age, race and ethnic group, sex, and language. That's just the beginning. To create and target products successfully, they are then broken down into lifestyles, location, gender orientation, preferences, diet, aversion to political rhetoric, you name it. Number of children, number of dogs, kind of car, type of music, favorite lipstick, age of personal computer, are all variables that are used in market segmentation.

This information is more than just trivia. It allows companies to zero in on who they can sell to and what they want to buy. Rather than trying to sell the proverbial "ice water to Eskimos," they sell it to people who really need it - Californians.

Some people believe that success in business has to do with your connections. They say, "It's not what you know, it's who you know." There is some truth to that. But from our experience with market segmentation, we believe success comes from the this principle:

"It's what you know about who you know."

If you want to successfully package and position your product, you should expand on your previous market research and segment the market. Let's do a sample market segmentation, breaking out the market based on three characteristics: physical attributes, job or responsibilities, and personality traits.

Prehistoric Market Segmentation: Cavemen

PHYSICAL	Breathing	No obvious diseases or wounds	Will produce strong off-spring
JOB	Light Fire	Get food	Kill Bears
CHARACTER	Doesn't bite	Picks fleas off of me	Doesn't Bite

As you can see, Groggette's view of her customer market was fairly basic - Get food, don't bite, try not to die. This cave woman was not waiting for Mr. Sits-Around-Like-Deer-Poop, she was interested in a person who was independent and trustworthy. In the same vein, Grog of the Opposable Thumbs was not looking for Ms. Always-Whining-Because-Me-Not-Taller. He was looking for someone who could have children and pick berries.

This worked for Neanderthals. You, however, are a bit more sophisticated in your tastes, and so is your target market. Here's a sample segmentation of the market for men in Dallas:

PHYSICAL	Kind of Big	Bigger Get food	Really Big Kill Bears
JOB	Works in Oil	Works with Cattle	Politician
CHARACTER	Gentlemanly	Rough and Rugged	Really Loud

32

Having completed the market analysis, you can now clearly see which of these segments is right for you (we're opting for the Big, Rough and Rugged Politician). What drives this decision is the segment size, attractiveness to you, and fit for the benefits and particulars of your product. One interesting exercise is to attempt to segment the market based on how you believe your target market would. This "turning upside down" of views gives a refreshing, and perhaps disturbing perspective on the problem.

Men's Perspective of How Women Perform Market Segmentation:

PHYSICAL	Will tolerate scrawny	Will tolerate beer gut	She wants muscles	She wants a big penis	She wants a WASP
JOB	No job / no money	Hard working blue collar	Hard working white collar	Professional	"ka-ching"
CHARACTER	Too nice	Makes me laugh	Reliable guy	Bad boy	Asshole jerk

Women's Perspective of How Men Perform Market Segmentation:

PHYSICAL	Brunette / redhead	Blond	Small thighs / large breasts	Large thighs / small breasts	Plastic fantasy woman
JOB	No job / no money	Factory / restaurant	Admin / clerical	Career professional	Mom
CHARACTER	Satisfactorily servile	Laid back / easy going	Buddies	Mysterious and unreachable	Bitch

There is probably an overlap of perception versus reality here, but one point is very clear. If you segment the market, accuracy counts. Otherwise you'll be aiming for Paris and hitting Podunk.

Dress It Up

So now you know exactly who you're going to target. The next step is to package your product. Product packaging can have several meanings. Here are three that you should remember:

1. To enclose in a package or covering
2. To present in a manner that will increase public interest and appeal
3. To fit into a package (or bundle of services)

Packaging is essentially the "dressing up" of the product. Call it the "Cinderella Effect." One day she's a dirty, coal-raking commoner, then dress her up in a nice pair of ill-fitting glass slippers and Voila - Prince bait.

How we dress, how we speak, how we eat, what we eat, what we like, and what we do are all visible elements of our product packages. The reason why so many of us have a favorite shirt, dress, shoes, pants, coat or even glasses is not just because of the style, but because of how flattering they are on us when we wear them.

Don't get carried away. Don't just start throwing on everything that you think looks good on you, or that your ex complimented you on. A good product package needs to have four elements. First, they need to be practical. If you look good in hiking boots but you're going to a catered wedding, the boots aren't practical. If high heels make your butt look firm and shapely, but your job requires you to walk the equivalent of five miles every day, the heels aren't practical. Wearing a tuxedo every day isn't practical either, unless you are a maitre d'.

Second, your package needs to be affordable. If your product is you, and you are broke because you spent your money on something that was too expensive, then your product is starting to become defective. That is, when someone opens the expensive package they're going to find a pretty cheap gift.

Third, your package needs to be consistent with the product. Every brunette can't be a redhead, every bozo can't be James Bond. Don't stray too far from the core strengths of the product. Promising "makes you feel good" when the product is "needs to feel good" is just asking for trouble.

Fourth, your package needs to be appealing to customers. You may like your package, it may reflect the inner you, it may be affordable and consistent, but if it doesn't attract your customers then the only buyer you'll have is yourself. As they say, "the person in love with themselves has no greater competition." This fourth element is the most difficult, because it requires us to look at our packaging from someone else's point of view. That is very, very hard to do. But, even if you're not successful, if you really sit down and think about it, you can identify whether you're moving in the right direction or not.

When I was in college I had a lot guys asking me out, and I always wore baggy sweat pants and sweat shirts. After I graduated though and went to work, hardly anyone ever wanted to get together. I thought is was "the real world," until one day a guy friend said that he had absolutely no idea why I dressed like I was trying to hide my body. I said that this is what I liked, and what I always wore. His response was, "Well, it kind of makes you look like a kid."

Since I wasn't really a kid, and wasn't trying to date any kids, I put all of those sweats at the bottom of my closet.

When people think of packaging themselves, they think of stylish duds and sexy outfits. They say, "I can dress up and look good." This is true, but sexy and fancy outfits are not the only way to package a product. In fact, the point is not to wrap it up everyday in the fanciest or most expensive designs, it is to wrap it up everyday in a way that accentuates and illustrates its unique assets. Let's say that again: Accentuates and illustrates your unique assets. If you have a nice bright set of teeth, the packaging could be as simple as actually smiling more often. If you have a rather unextraordinary derriere, but know that your target market is attracted to derrieres, turn to Brazilian and French fashion for ways to make it look like it's a 10 (believe us, they know - they really, really, know). If you been told that you have nice hands, keep your nails trimmed and groomed. If you have a largesse of physique, work to make it look alluring instead of unhealthy.

On the subject of largesse, a lot of people would like to know how to be more attractive. The obvious answer is to lose weight and work out, and this is the one that most people will give. It is good advice, especially for longevity and ease of advertising. But, it doesn't work for everyone, and then you have to work with what you've got.

Our observation is that there are two kinds of large in bodies. There is a *large* which appears to the general public that the person can't stop eating, sweats all the time, and would not be particularly attractive in bed. These people often package themselves in clothing and fashion that add to the negative perception. It looks like they are so large that they can't get their clothes to fit. Our advice is that there is always a clothing size that fits. Don't wear clothing that is extremely tight, since unless we're talking about breasts you're not necessarily accentuating the best assets, and even then ONLY if you're a woman. Conversely, don't wear clothing that is extremely loose because you'll look like a walking garbage bag. Your goal is to package yourself as the second, more attractive, large-person body type. This consists of people who don't look obese, they look ample, they don't look blubbery, they look powerful, they don't look like their oral appetites are out of control, they look like their sensual appetites are uncontrollable. Is this a dream description? No, not at all. Take a survey. Give yourself a month, and really ask around. There will be people who are quite large that others will unexpectedly point out as unquestionably attractive. Find them. Observe them. Hell, go up and talk to them. Discover their secret. Size is not always an obstacle. This is the packaging that you want.

Personality is more important than appearance

It goes without saying that if you are dirty, un-hygienic, and fashionably ridiculous, your appearance is going to get in the way of your personality. Negative external packaging prevents potential customers from sampling the product, and you have to make sure that this doesn't happen. But make sure that your core packaging is based on the value of your personality. Personality makes people notice you. Personality makes people interested in you. Personality is why average looking people are often seen with above-average looking spouses. It's not always their careers, or money, or sexual prowess that lands those catches, it's their personalities.

The same is true in business. If you walk into a meeting looking meek and demure, no one will pay attention to you, unless you happen to be the CEO. If you go into a meeting being loud, boisterous, cocky, and over-confident, people will be attentive yet annoyed and threatened. You have to seek a balance. You need to make a good impression by being confident and assured, yet not convinced that no one can withstand your charms. You have to be interesting, while showing that you are interested.

Some people attempt to make an impression by trying to be funny. Humor is a major tool in the personality game, and it works very well, most of the time. You don't have to be a standup comic to be successful, you just need to avoid certain topics so that you don't accidentally ruin your chances.

1) Don't joke about your date's gender quirks

2) Don't joke about your ex or past dates

3) Don't joke about other people's religions, races, ethnicity, or language (you can joke about their food, however)

4) Don't joke about sex, porn, soft-porn, or sexualized parts of a person's body (i.e. breasts, butts, penises, thighs, feet, etc.)

5) Don't tell any jokes that you have recently heard unless you are ABSOLUTELY positive that your date won't find them offensive (when in doubt, don't)

6) Don't joke about your dates choices (dinner, decoration, clothing, career, car, ex, etc.)

These aren't very hard rules to follow. There are a lot of ways to be funny without putting someone else down. Especially, since you want to make sure that you don't put down by accident the person in which you are interested.

True personality comes from doing, from having done. "Doing" is an active sport. Even reading is more active than doing nothing, plus it has the benefit of creating something to discuss. Read a good book. Read the newspaper. Read a magazine. Turn off the television and read. Being able to say, "I read something interesting the other day," is a very powerful indication that you actually have a personality.

Another way to demonstrate personality is to have a life. Have things to do, things that interest you. Pursue those interests. Different is good. As we've said, most people are looking for common areas between them, but aren't looking for clones. They are looking for spice. Spice is what you add to all of your regular ingredients to either enhance their flavor or create an entirely new taste. You should be "spice." Having your own life, with your own interests, is one way for you to generate spice. By being "spice" you can help your date take the same ingredients and make them better. They can do the same for you.

Good spice always balances other flavors. It doesn't detract, it adds. As a good spice, you should try to stay positive rather than negative. In some regions of the world (i.e. New York City) a liberal sprinkling of negative comments in a conversation is part of the culture - "It sure sucks out here, you know?" "Yup, it sure does, and the damn bus is late again." Avoid the temptation to be negative in your conversations with a date. Positive is always more attractive than negative, even if the world, the stock market, and your life are falling apart.

Listening

Listening is one of the sexiest things that you can do. It shows that you are interested in the other person, and interest is very attractive. When a person has the opportunity to tell you about their likes, hobbies, and what they do for fun, they are essentially giving you an open window into their personal business plan. The fact that you want to hear it is extremely appealing.

Not a lot of dates actually listen to each other. They either talk solely about themselves, talk about topics irrelevant to the other person, or don't talk enough. Listening is a good way to know how to balance these three problem areas. When you listen well, you have an opportunity to answer questions about yourself in a way that ties into the topics talked about by your date. You start to know subjects in which they are interested, and you aren't tempted to simply sit like a bump-on-a-log and be intimidatingly unentertaining.

In business school as in life, interviewing for a job is a routine experience. Many people jump right in and tell the interviewer what they want in a position, and ask what's in it for them. Other people sit and listen quietly until asked questions and allowed to speak. We have found that one successful interviewing method is based on listening. Start the interview by asking about the needs of the company, a description of the problem or situation, what is being looked for in a candidate, and how the search is progressing (any likely candidates). After they have finished answering, you can tailor all of the future discussion so that it hones in on the points they brought up, fitting your strengths and experience to their issues, and essentially positioning yourself as a perfect candidate who really understands their needs. This method works very well in second date situations.

Listening is a two-way street. If both people on a date listen to each other, they actually get to know one another. This is partially the purpose of dating - research. Who are they? What do they like? What do I like about them? What could they like about me? If you go on a date and haven't actually shared some level of information that helps reach these conclusions, then your date really didn't happen. Fun may have happened, sex may have happened, heavy drinking may have happened, but an actual "date" did not happen. You were just hanging out with a new buddy.

Ask questions, make eye contact, hear their responses, try not to be too distracted by your surroundings (or for more men especially, by other potential dates).

Here's a good listening exercise, taken from the comedic technique called "reincorporation." In improvisational comedy, where you have to take spontaneous events and topics and create a humorous presentation in front of a live audience, the technique of reincorporation is highly utilized. What they do is watch very closely previous skits and improvs taking place during the show, the topics and jokes and subjects, and then reincorporate these into their own skit, even if it's on a completely different issue. This weaving of past subjects into current material creates a common comedic point of reference, a recognized subject line, and makes the current skit even funnier to audience, who all get the joke. We're not saying that you should try to be a stand-up comic to prove that you are listening, but we are recommending that you take a page from the improvisational handbook and practice the art of reincorporation to enhance your listening skills, as well as to make your date more interesting.

Remember, the point of packaing is not to prove that you can push your wares just like everyone else, it is to push your stuff *past* everyone else. Figure out what you're trying to sell before you decide on the packaging. Come up with a list, then match your selections to those items. Sell the steak, not the sizzle.

Common Product Packaging for Dating

Preppy / Yuppie / Professional Business person	Non-materialistic (poor) creative type	Well-dressed (rich) artistic type	Dedicated (fanatical) sports fan
Athletic & Health-Conscious Gym Groupie and Jogger	Jersey Girl/Island Girl/ Indiana Girl/Valley Girl	Urban	Suburban
Casual yet conservative	Casual yet non-conservative	The Hippies of this Era	The Fascists of this Era
I haven't a clue how to dress because no one who had a clue ever passed it on to me	Hey, check out the T&A	I don't dress up because I'm not into that shit, so take it or leave pal	Why, do I stand out?
I like Megadeath	I like Stevie Nicks	I like Tunisian folklore music	I like my computer ... a lot

Packaging Case Study: Madonna

Superstar Madonna Louise Veronica Ciccone was born in Rochester, Michigan, in 1958. Young Madonna liked to sing and dance, and her aspirations to "be famous" were no different than millions of other girls around the world. But Madonna succeeded where others failed, and Madonna's enterprises have fueled popular trends in fashion, music, dance, sex, gender orientation, yoga, and women still going to the gym past the age of 40. Also, because of her power, fame, and sexual adventurousness, Madonna apparently can get any man, or woman, that she wants (with exception of Spanish actor Antonio Banderas, who was looking for a really All-American girl when he decided to leave his faithful Spanish wife). She could therefore be considered a role model for all of us.

Over the years she has become closely associated with many cultural expressions, including "Material Girl," "Boy Toy," "Trend-Following Chameleon," and "Shape-Shifting Provocateur." There is no doubt that she finds a new product trend and claims it as her own.

How did Madonna Louise Veronica Ciccone become the one-word supernova known as Madonna? She did it through a superior packaging strategy.

Chronology of Madonna

1978 - Madonna Ciccone left a dancing scholarship and dropped out of college.

1982 - Madonna scores her first club scene hit, "Everybody." She follows those with Top 40 hits "Holiday," "Lucky Star," and "Borderline." Her raunchy, haltered-topped, blond-dyed, mid-rift exposed look becomes imitated by teenage girls around the globe. Madonna is officially packaged as a "bad girl."

1984-1987 - Realizing it's good to be bad, Madonna releases her next album. Madonna appears at a music awards show dressed in a white bridal gown singing her new song, "Like a Virgin." Madonna commences to slink across the stage, seduce the audience, and hump the floor in a decidedly non-virgin manner. Madonna is now a cutting-edge, slightly scandalous, very well-known pop act. In 1985 she gets real naughty by marrying bad boy, Sean Penn. Madonna sees that Latin music will eventually make it into mainstream pop, and records the song, "La Isla Bonita," laying the foundation for her future "Spanish-flavored" packaging. She has also created a secondary persona in which she casts herself as the horny and materialistic reincarnation of Marilyn Monroe. This means that Madonna can dress down as well as up without confusing her fans, and at times is seen on stage wearing glamorous evening gowns. She is now packaged as a "very bad girl with expensive tastes."

1989 - Trying to prove that she can make the public forget all of her bad films (Vision Quest, Goose and Tom-Tom, Shanghai Surprise, Who's that Girl?), she goes for the jugular vein of controversy with her "Like a Prayer" video, in which a scanty Madonna dances in front of burning crosses, kisses a non-Italian saint, and spouts stigmata. The Pope, Vatican, and Pepsi are pissed. Madonna stays in the spotlight, ending the eighties and starting the nineties as an apostle of hedonism. She is now packaged as a "very, very bad girl, but one who is becoming self-empowered." Madonna's got balls.

1990-1992 - Continuing to advance her product positioning philosophy of "any press is good press," Madonna decides that the '90's are a time of erotic freedom, and as Columbus supposedly discovered the "new world", she has discovered sex. Madonna let's the world share in her new image as sexual liberator by releasing an album ("Erotica"), book ("Sex"), video ("Justify My Love"), and clothing designer (Galliano and his pointed leather bondage bras) on the theme. She also becomes buddies with well-known New York divas Debbie Mazar, Sandra Bernhard, and Rosie O'Donnell (with whom she appears in a hit movie about women in baseball). Sandra is not only tough and funny, she's also bisexual, which is perfect for Madonna's new product message of sexual exploration. She openly advocates girl-on-girl pleasure in her videos, and positions herself as now possibly bisexual, though no one knows for sure. The mystery is enticing, and we watch her closely to see if there's a closet from which she'll emerge. Eventually the public tires of the lack of clarity, as the Artist Formerly Known as Prince and Michael Jackson have done this bit to death. Madonna slowly moves on to other packaging, leaving her new best friends to their own devices. As Madonna moves from friend to friend and image to image, one emerging theme is that if you talk badly about Madonna in public your ass is in hot water, as ostracization from the Magnificent One will close a lot of doors on you permanently. Even tough talking no-nonsense celebs are very careful about what they say on the "private life" of the Material Girl. This, at least, intrigues us.

1991-1992 - Madonna studies the improvisational and unique dance movements of New York City's "Vogueing" gay and transvestite community, and incorporates their manner of dress, speaking, and formality into her repertoire. Most of these dancers are poor, Black, and Hispanic, and spend a large amount of time and energy grooming themselves to perfection as part of the "vogue." Having mastered these movements, Madonna packages herself as semi-Hispanic, and recruits several voguers to appear in the video of her new song, appropriately entitled, "Vogue." In the video, Madonna not only sings about attitude, she dedicates the song to classic movie stars who she says had it, thus raising herself to their level and reinforcing her ongoing positioning as the new Marilyn Monroe. The entire concert road tour connected to the song is filmed, including non-performance parts such as backstage preparation, practices, Madonna's love life with aging sex symbol Warren Beatty, her relationship with her dancers, the moments when she gets pissed, etc. She releases the edited tape as a documentary called "Truth or Dare", which is praised by the critics, and fascinates the public. Madonna comes across as a talented, driven, in-control, bitchy, hard-working genius. After the tour in 1996, Madonna has a baby by her choreographer, who is Hispanic.

1993-1995 - Customer over saturation has occurred. We are really damn tired of looking at Madonna. We know it, she knows it, and she disappears for a long enough time that we forget it. Her unplanned positioning at the time was "very annoying and overexposed not-as-baaaaad-as-she-thinks girl."

1996 - Madonna is Evita Peron, famous Latin First Lady of a fallen Argentinean dictatorship. The rags-to-riches-to-rags tale, whose story arc includes love and worship of Evita by her millions of countrymen, is a perfect Madonna packaging vehicle. It solidifies her queen-like status in the mind of the everyman. At some point we realize that Madonna is no longer possibly bi-sexual, especially since entertainers are coming out of the closet in droves as 100% gay. Obviously, Madonna can no longer claim the competitive advantage of being "cutting-edge" on this issue.

Around 1997 & 1998 - Where does a real Queen live? England. 'Let's see what all this Queen stuff is really about,' Madonna says. Madonna is now a respectable mother, and can't seriously raise a child and still be portrayed as a teenage tramp, especially since she's far from being a teenager anymore. Time to Get Out of Dodge. Madonna moves to England, where she falls in love with the country, realizes that they have a cutting-edge music scene which greatly influences the rest of the world, and decides that she is now English. Her accent changes, her vocabulary changes, and for the word 'schedule' she now says the British "shed-u-al" instead of the American "sked-u-al." Everything is now "quite" this and "quite" that, and she starts delving into the world of techno/ambient-dance music, the current rage across Europe. Madonna becomes a techno/ambient music Queen, and packages her new album and videos to reflect that. Now over 40, Madonna has proven that she still is "with it," and appeals to club-going music lovers of all ages, especially the age where you do a lot of Ecstasy.

2000 - Madonna marries a British film director in a Scottish castle in her version of a "Material Girl's fairy-tale". Despite the fact that she had his child before the wedding, she is now packaged as a "deep & spiritual person of substance." Madonna can move in and out of British society and nobility with ease, as well as drop down into the local dance joint to shake her still firm booty. Few people remember where she was born, and by the way she talks it's hard to believe they care (or have the nerve to remind her). She has now arrived as a premium brand.

Conclusion: Two key product marketing principles can be learned from Madonna's career. The first is that over time you need to adjust your product's positioning and packaging as much as required to keep your customer's interest, as long as you don't change it radically in a short period of time. In fact, you can go from "boy toy" to "queen" in the span of a few years.

The second is that even though sex sells, it can be overdone. Don't' worry, though. It's unlikely that you will have that problem.

Beware of Trademarks

Some people confuse "trademarks" with proper packaging. They say, "The Artist Formerly and Currently Known as Prince has a trademark look, Mariah Cary has a trademark look, and biologically-enhanced 'actress' Pamela Sue Andersen has a trademark look. They're glamorous. They're famous. I can have a trademark look too."

Not a very good idea. These people truly are products, like Spic & Span, Mop & Glo, and Polo shirts. They are packaged and sold to millions of people, and their personal styles reflect that mass market impact. Like many consumer products, their promoters want the audience to be able to quickly identify them via a certain symbol, value, or style. You may argue that Prince isn't mass market, but that can't be completely true since far more than one thousand people purchase his albums. You, on the other hand, are not a mass market product and are targeting a lot less than one thousand people. For that reason, creating a trademark look that appeals to the masses is a wasted, and particularly embarrassing, effort.

I knew a woman who only dressed in purple. Purple boots, purple pants, purple sweaters, and purple hats, all at the same time. Then she'd accessorize them with purple belts, purple purses, purple knapsacks, and purple coats.

The first time you saw her you were like, "Wow. She really knows how to coordinate her look. Who is that woman? What's her name?"

But it got old pretty fast. After a while you were like, "Do you have anything else to wear?" I mean, sometimes when she was wearing a purple down parka she looked just like a big walking grape. You're kind of like, "Girl, what have you been smoking?"

Not all trademark grooming styles are as extreme as purple-mania. However, they can be as annoying and detrimental to your dating health.

I dated a girl once who was really into long-sleeved, white cotton shirts. We'd go to the movie: long-sleeved, white cotton shirt. We'd go to a nice restaurant: long-sleeved, white cotton shirt. We'd go to a black-tie charity fund-raiser: long-sleeved, white cotton shirt.

I'm a guy, and sometimes I don't really notice when someone wears clothes more than once. Heck, half the time I'm hoping no one will notice when I wear the same thing twice. But this lady was wearing the same kind of shirt every time we got together. In fact, for all I know it may have been the same shirt.

I finally just said, "It seems like you really like that shirt. I think I've seen it before."

Then she says, "Yeah, I like it because it's comfortable."

Whatever. The last thing I need is someone who's obsessive.

One man's obsession is another's comfortable shoes. Here's one more example:

I dated a guy who only wore plaid shirts. This would have been OK if we lived in Oklahoma, but this was Chicago, and we both worked downtown. You could see him coming three blocks away: red and black, green and black, orange and black.

I once asked if he grew up on a farm, or liked to hike, or was of Scottish ancestry. "Nope," he said.

Another time I asked him to go shopping with me, and offered to buy him a new shirt at Marshall Fields. We went to the Men's section, and he walked straight over to the first plaid shirts he saw.

I figured if this guy can be that locked into one style that he won't consider changing, I'm going to have a hard time getting him to experience anything new.

As you can see, sometimes what has become a trademark originated simply as a innocent personal grooming choice, but later they become competitive disadvantages. Actor/Director/Producer Ron Howard is known for his baseball caps. Everywhere he goes, whether it's the Oscars or Scala, Ron is seen wearing a baseball cap. Does Ron have a trademark style? Yes. Did Ron need one to package and promote himself? No. Ron wears a baseball cap everywhere because Ron is bald. Once known for his sparky red hair, Ron now has a shiny scalp that he conscientiously conceals beneath a hat. No one blames him. Millions of balding men around the world would love to be able to wear a hat all the time. Unfortunately, they're not Ron Howard.

As you can see, trademarks tend to develop from need. I need to be different, I need to be comfortable, I need to hide my bald spot. But they're a double-edged sword. They tell the world that you are different all right, but not different in a fascinating way. Maybe at first, and that's enough to lure in your potential customers, but not enough to keep them. What once attracted can quickly repel. Trademarks are tricky, tricky tools best left to experts. Here's another example of a trademark gone bad:

Michael Jackson was my favorite star in the '70's. He and the Jackson Five were too cool. They had the afros, the bell bottom pants, and the dance moves. The guy could sing. Remember "ABC"? Right on, baby!

I loved his "Off the Wall" album. It rocked. "I'm gonna rock the night with you... dance you into sunlight!" I know all the songs. That album was a big hit.

Then in about '82 he came out with "Thriller," and that had a lot of good stuff. Some of it was even controversial at the time, especially for Michael. "What's up with that song 'Billy Jean'? Did Michael have an illegitimate child? And in that song 'PYT' he's talking about 'Pretty Young Things.'" But hey, it was Michael JACKSON. He was a superstar.

Then he started wearing that glove on his hand. Just one glove, not two. Sometimes with fingers, sometimes with sequins. You're like, "What's up with the glove, Mike?" But he kept making hits.

Then he started changing color. You could see it right before your eyes. It was OK when he made his nose smaller, because it looked good, at least when he started. But when he started changing color, it was too much. He was like a big Transformer action figure. "Now he's Black, Now's he's not. Now he has a wide nose, now he has a

44

collapsed nose. Now he has normal eyes, now he has eyes like Diana Ross with too much mascara." And all the time, he's still wearin' that damn glove. It's like the glove was the only part of him that didn't change. Like we needed that glove just to remember who we were lookin' at.

We were like, "Uhh, who the hell is that? Is it human? Oh, wait a minute. It's got one glove on. Must be Michael Jackson. Damn, Michael is really fucked up."

The bottom line is that you can have a style. You can have favorite colors and hats and shirts and stuff. You can have a favorite band or artist or chair. But you absolutely have to change it up sometime. Throw in something different, something new. Otherwise you eventually scare the crap out of people.

Assume the Position

You've got the product, you've got the package, but how do you position it in the market so that it compares favorably with the competition? How do you say, "This is what you get baby when you buy one of these"?

Product positioning involves identifying, creating and communicating a message that can establish and differentiate the company or brand in relation to competitors.

An example is that Macintosh computers have been positioned as the "easiest to use", and IBM has been positioned as the "industry standard." BMW has been positioned as a "highly engineered luxury vehicle," while Porsche is considered the "highly aerodynamic luxury sports car."

There is often more than one feature or dimension in which products can claim superiority. Firms must be careful, however, not to stretch their credibility by claiming to be the "best in the world", or for that matter, the best in everything.

Whatever the product claims, they must be in line with what customers do or could perceive based on advertising, packaging, word of mouth, or actual experience.

How would you position yourself? Obviously you'd want to take some combination of competitive advantages and market segmentation to develop an appropriate positioning strategy. As we mentioned in earlier chapters, under the right conditions you could position yourself as "model-esque." Or if you like sports you could position yourself as "athletic." If you like to read, you might position yourself as "literary" or "sophisticated." And if you like to go out every night to raves and dance until 6 am you could position yourself as "a serious party-er."

Examine how your positioning compares you to the competition. Does it make you "of equal strength" or does it make you "superior." Either of those may be adequate for the situation. Under other circumstances, being able to successfully position oneself as "not so bad" is a major success, especially considering the product. "Not so bad" can get you in the running, particularly when for other reasons your product is the best alternative to going home alone.

Positioning is serious business. McDonald's and Burger King have been fighting the Positioning Wars for years. McDonald's has "special sauce," while Burger King has "flame-broiled." Burger King claims greater customer service in that you can "have it your way," while McDonald's offers you a cozy home away from home where you can meet friends, family, your softball team after too many beers, or a date. As petty as they sound, these various positioning strategies have kept both enterprises profitable and at the top for decades.

How are you positioning yourself when you go out with your friends? Are you "the leader" of the pack," or are you "the shy one" of the group? Are you "the funny guy," or are you "the all-American male"? The "librarian" or the "libertarian"? As they used to say in the '50's, "what's your angle?"

For those who lack an angle, or product positioning strategy, here are a few you might consider:

- Morally motivated
- Open-minded
- Conservatively-oriented
- Family-oriented
- Looking to settle down
- Looking to bust out
- Recently divorced
- Recently broken-up
- Recently paid
- Easy to know
- Easy to trust
- Just plain easy
- Prudish
- Stuffy
- Immature
- Spoiled
- Spoiled rotten
- "I know I'm hot, and so does everyone"
- Annoying
- Entertaining
- The rock and roll guru
- Inexperienced yet willing
- The hip-hop shaman
- The Animal Rights Crusader
- The "last person to leave a party"
- An upwardly mobile person
- Solid and Stable

46

- Confident and self-assured
- A "Major Player"
- A Networking Machine
- "I know everyone here, let me introduce you to my friends"
- Artistically inspired
- Creative
- A solidly built sex machine
- Highly motivated, a "go-getter"
- Rich in spirit
- Rich in currency
- Just off the farm
- Escaped from the Convent
- "Buy me a drink and I may talk to you"
- Surfer-esque
- Hardest working
- Able to make a commitment

Dating's Classic Failure

Before you jump right in and decide on your positioning, you need to know that some ideas have been done, and done badly. Avoid them. Stay away. You are wasting your time. The following are three really bad positioning concepts:

Classic Positioning Failure #1: "The Good Friend"

Dependable but not necessarily exciting, that's you. "But I'm here, I'm a good friend, and you WILL one day find me attractive." Dream on, baby. Not even your dullest, most dim-witted friends are going to fall for that one. With luck you may catch them in a weak moment and have a one-nighter, or even get in on some rebound action. But we all know the *Big Plan* is for them to say, "Hey, I liked that, let's start dating." You've got less chance of this happening than you do of meeting an ostrich in aerobics, and in this case we recommend you focus your energy on the ostrich. That isn't to say you should not be a nice and dependable person, because you should. These are desirable personality traits. We also are not saying that a good date can't become a good friend. They can, and hopefully they will. We're just saying that a good platonic friend isn't likely to get a date, ever, so stop trying.

Classic Positioning Failure #2: "The 'Ba-a-a-d' Friend"

The problem here is that you need to stay 'ba-a-a-ad' to stay interesting. But of course then you're not taken seriously as a long-term romantic prospect. Sure, there may be some crushes and curiosity, but in the long-run they won't consider you as the relationship-type. You are too ba-a-a-ad, too free. Still, you might score a few good one-night stands with this approach.

Classic Positioning Failure #3: "The Needy Friend"

Oh yeah, just what everyone needs, more baggage. Good friends should be there to help you out. They may even sleep with you if you give them a chance. But they have already seen your whiny side, and it doesn't say to their romantic side, "Yum, yum, yum, that looks like a fun date." For more explanation on why not, read on.

Always Sell Upwards

One tip about Dating and positioning. Unless you are looking for someone to play the hero, never willingly position yourself as the victim. The role of "saved" victim brings a lot of baggage and expectations with it, and once you go there the road away from it is long and painful. In the last two decades, almost every business that's been "saved" by a white knight has been dismembered, broken up, leveraged, mortgaged, and downsized. Sometimes you really are the victim, but imagine if those businesses were you.

Author Tama Janowitz hit the nail on the head with the title of her hit book, "Slaves of New York." Her series of interconnecting short stories was built on the premise that in New York, relationships are partly built on need, and the needier person, particularly if they need to shack up with their date because they don't have a place to live, the more they are a slave to their companion.

What you really want to aim at in your positioning is the sweet spot on Maslow's Hierarchy of Needs. Abraham Maslow created a theory about human behavior based on the premise that human beings are motivated by unsatisfied needs, and that certain lower needs have to be satisfied before higher ones can be addressed. He believed that people are essentially loving, growing, trustworthy, and self-governing. People become anti-social and violent when their human needs aren't met. The overall set of needs, however, is what motivates us towards growth, or a state of "Self-Actualization."

So, if you don't have somewhere to live and its raining all the time, your base need is to find a dry place. Or if you feel like all your dates end with the person looking out the window bored silly, your base need is for one to end with great conversation and laughter.

As Maslow put it, when your base needs are met:

> At once other (and higher) needs emerge, and these, rather than physi-
> ological hungers, dominate the organism. And when these in turn are
> satisfied, again new (and still higher) needs emerge, and so on. As
> one desire is satisfied, another pops up to take its place.

There is no doubt that the planners of the American consumer-based free market system understood Maslow very well. Without those continual needs to get the next great thing, the economy sputters like a fish sucking on grapefruit.

Maslow has four categories of human needs required to reach Self Actualization (S.A.). They are Physiological Needs, Safety Needs, Love Needs, and Esteem Needs.

Physiological needs are as basic as you can get: food, water, sleep, air, sex, etc. When you don't get these you're pretty irritable and unhealthy. In fact, until they are satisfied you can't think of anything else. This is one good explanation why it's so hard to get teenage boys to think about their homework.

Safety needs are based on creating and finding consistency and stability in this crazy, mixed up world. You are looking for mental security. You need to feel like you have family and friends, like you belong somewhere and that people care about you. People need to feel like there is law and order, even within their own households. If someone is always screaming at you whenever they speak, you lack that feeling of security. Or if a person is always changing their mind about your relationship, one day in it, one day not sure, one day in it, the next ready to leave, you lack the satisfaction of your safety needs. You can't move up to the next level.

Love needs are based on another type of belonging, in a non-sexual context. We need to feel like we "belong." Starting a new job, joining clubs and fraternities, or maybe even becoming more religious are ways in which this need is addressed by some. Cheering for a particular professional sports team is another way that we may choose to belong, even if it's to a greater, impersonal group.

Yes, all those strong, macho sports-aholics are simply looking for Love.

Esteem needs are based on both competence at a task, as well as attention and recognition from others. Another level of belonging, we are now seeking admiration instead of simple acceptance. We want to have some power over others, as they admire our accomplishments. There are many ways that people address their needs for esteem. They can learn to dance really well. They can buy designer clothes. They can drive a phallic red sports car. They can run for President. They can even give a good speech at the PTA. The admiration and recognition they receive address their needs for esteem.

Esteem should not be confused with "self-esteem." Maslow's Esteem Need is based on the attention of others, not on you trying to respect yourself. Not respecting yourself is not an "Esteem" need, it's a Physiological & Safety need. If you have issues with self-esteem, we recommend you return to Levels and I & II and don't pass Go.

Self-Actualization is 'the desire to become more and more what one is, as well as to become all that one is capable of becoming.' Self-actualized persons look for new levels, they seek knowledge, they want peace and serenity, they search for new experiences and self-fulfillment. Doesn't that sound attractive? It is indeed very attractive. This is one reason why the wealthy appear very seductive to certain people. It is believed that with all of their basic needs filled they can actively pursue these higher level ones. It's also why peasants, slaves, and serfs had a difficult time becoming self-actualized, they were too busy with the food and water issue. You, on the other hand, can go the route of becoming self-actualized, or at least appearing in the process of, and your level of attraction will increase exponentially.

A word of caution. Don't be fooled by "self-actualization" posers. If someone tells you that they "have to find themselves," wish them good luck and send the out the door. The difference between a person "in the process of finding themselves" and a person who "has to or is trying to find themselves" is the difference between a person wanting "to do well at a job" and a person wanting "well, a job." One is on their way there, the other has just started. Stick with the person who's not at the "startup" stage.

Many celebrities have packaged themselves as self-actualized. Jane Fonda, Shirley McClain, John Lennon, Madonna, Bono, Ricki Martin, Richard Gere, these are all celebrities who do some yoga, talk to the Dali Lama, fight for an acre of land in the Siberian eco-system, raise money for their favorite charity, or study Jewish mysticism, and appear to have their act together. One could argue that you should admire them for their progress. In fact, by the simple fact that they are becoming enlightened and are celebrities, and by providing good role models, it could be argued that they are inspiring you to move up the rungs of self-actualization.

Of course, many people see a good, self-actualized role model as one who sports a big diamond ring, buys a large house in the Hamptons, and drives the latest expensive car with optional tinted windows. As is always the case, it's all about knowing your target market.

The reason why we bring up Maslow's Hierarchy of Needs is that based on our own experiences we truly believe that the best dates are the ones that are at the Love level of Self-Actualization or above. At least they package and position themselves that way. They don't start the relationship with, "I don't have anything decent to eat in my house. I'm away from my family and I'm lonely. I can't get enough sleep because I work too much. My car is two years old and I

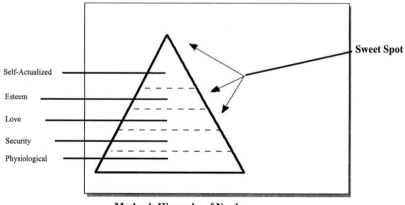

Self-Actualized

Esteem

Love

Security

Physiological

Sweet Spot

Maslow's Hierarchy of Needs

50

want a new one." These issues are turn-offs because they require too much maintenance. People don't want high-maintenance situations thrown at them. If these truly are unmet needs, good dates fake it. They don't let you know. They avoid the topic. They say, "Hey, if we get to that stage in our relationship where this person could actually help me address those needs, then I'll bring it up." They don't sell downwards. They go for the low-maintenance Sweet Spot: Love Needs, Esteem Needs, and Self-Actualization.

Product Messaging

Developing the appropriate product messaging is important to the success of your business plan. Without it, what you communicate about your product to your customers will essentially vary inconsistently from moment to moment and situation to situation. The market will be confused, and so will you.

There are easy steps that you can take to create these messages. First, develop a mission statement. In a brief format of one to two paragraphs, define and write down the answers to the questions of what you are, what your objectives are and how you do business. This should be a vision of you as a business. The mission statement will help you stay true to this vision, even as you encounter new opportunities and challenges.

For you, a sample mission statement might be:

"We will deliver to the customer first-class products that will delight
and satisfy their needs and desires. We will always stand behind our
partners, and quickly communicate to them any changes in thrust and
direction. We will be tough and competitive, working to overcome all
obstacles to the ultimate climax of our objectives."

or,

"I am very desirable to the right person, and that person will find me
to be the most attractive, intelligent, funny, and sexy person they've
ever gone out with. I will find that person within the next 12 months,
and when I do they will want to spend so much time together that
we will eventually get married. But not before we have a lot of fun
with the Kama Sutra."

or,

"I am awesome, and I want as many people as possible to know that
I'm awesome."

or,

"My aim is to save the world and stop war, famine, and poverty. I want to find a mate who will join me in achieving these goals. I will empower myself by cleansing my body and chi with revitalizing VitaBetaBod supplements, taken three times a day."

or,

"I am not boring. I am very interesting. Everyone else is stupid. My objective is to enlighten them to that fact."

Obviously, choosing the right mission statement is key to achieving your objectives.

The next step is to prepare your key messages. These are the persuasive product points and benefits that you want continually communicated in all of your efforts. For example, the key messages of many technology products are often the following:

•Lower Costs
•Higher Efficiency (requires less hand holding)
•Powerful (fast)
•Scalable (can handle the load of 1 to 10,000 people)
•Robust (won't crash every time you ask it to do something)
•Integrates with industry standards (works with Microsoft, Sun, and Oracle products)

An "elevator pitch" can be developed from these messages. An "elevator pitch" is a description of a company or product that can be delivered in the amount of time you have to tell someone while standing in a moving elevator. This time varies from 10 seconds to 30. For that reason some people call it a "30-second" pitch. These "pitches" are extremely useful because in reality one rarely has as much time as one would like to extol the virtues of a product. Often you just have to get to the point as quickly as possible. Hence the "elevator pitch."

For the products above, there would usually be pages of literature that describe how they are used, the system requirements, software versions, etc. But an elevator pitch might sound like the following:

"Our X9000 series [high tech widgets] provide companies with the ability to lower costs due to its high level of efficiency. Because its one of the most powerful, robust and scalable [high tech widgets] on the market users can perform their [activities] better than before. Plus, you can leverage your investment in other products because the X9000 integrates with industry standards."

Wow. Got to get one of those.

The good news is that the person who heard this is now either interested, because they might be able to use one of these and wants to hear more, or are not interested because they already have a good product and this one doesn't really sound significantly better...or the delivery of the pitch sucked.

Think about how you could use a thirty second pitch. Or more specifically, think about how your friends, family, and associates could use a nice thirty-second pitch about you, supplied by you. Certainly they think they already have one, but it's probably the equivalent of:

> "The X9000 is really nice, because it doesn't cost a lot and doesn't break down all the time. It can handle a lot of stress without going to pieces, and won't require you to get rid of the other things you've got. "

Not too appealing, is it?

Fortunately you don't to live with that drivel. Armed with a thirty-second pitch and messages created and supplied by you, this ragtag group of people can become your unofficial advertising agency and sales force.

Sample Messages to Try

> "His ex says that he's a fantastic person, and great in bed"

> "A lot of people have been waiting a long time for her to come back on the market "

Kiss-of-Death Messages to Avoid at All Costs

> "She's nice"

> "He's really nice"

> "She likes to party"

> "He lives with his mother"

FAQs

When you want to really cover your bases, it's best to provide an FAQ as well. FAQ stands for the official answers to Frequently Asked Questions. For example, "How do they look?", "What do they do?", "How tall are they?", "How old are they?", and "Why are they still single?" are all Frequently Asked Questions. Knowing this, you can prepare a set of standard answers that you and your team can rattle off earnestly yet non-chalantly, as they "inform and persuade" but don't "sell" the potential customer on your product. Often you want an FAQ so that you can fill in the details for the press and customers. Sometimes, you want to answer the question with an acceptable explanation, but not with the detailed facts, which might be quite negative. Remember, always answer FAQs in the positive. "The product won't be anywhere close to ready for two more years" can be answered "We anticipate delivery sometime over the next 12-18 months", and "This product tastes like my dog pee'd on it, and plus it makes a purple rash under your armpits" becomes "As many sophisticated consumers can attest, now you can enjoy at home a complex, earthy taste similar to the rare Chateau-Broullionette cheeses of France. Of course, if you are allergic to the rare Chateau-Broullionette cheese, you may experience a mild reaction." Be positive, positive, positive. Or at least, not so negative.

Make sure your FAQs work as expected by testing them out on friends. See if they can say the responses without laughing out loud or turning green with envy. Better yet, enlist them in writing your answers for you. From focus groups often come usable kernels of truth.

Sample FAQ (Frequently Asked Questions)

How do they look?
> They are "The Bomb"! I don't know exactly what it is, but everyone always thinks they're pretty hot. You know how some people are like that? They're not a model, you know, but they just look good.

How tall are they?
> About average. They've got a really nice body, it's in exact proportion with their height.

Where did they grow up ("go to school" is often substituted)
> I think a few different places. I heard that they spent some time in France, Hawaii, and Kenya (the truth is that they want to vacation there, but the speaker is only saying that "they heard", so it can't be taken as a statement of fact and therefore an untruth).

What do they do for a living?
> I think they're working to become a [insert something really cool, or very lucrative] They're very independent. I've never known them to have problems with money, or even ask anyone else to borrow some. I heard that they were really smart in [insert real or plausible area of expertise].

Where do they live?
> I can't remember the address, but I think they're not too far from you.

Would you date them?
> Absolutely! If we weren't [such good friends/coworkers/family/the wrong sex] I would definitely go out with them

Why are they still single?

They just returned from a trip to Australia, where they were helping UNICEF establish a new type of farm that grows rare plants for pharmaceuticals and doesn't destroy the rain forest. They probably won't be single for too long though, because they seem to have a way of really attracting [men/women]. It's not that they're looking for a long term commitment, but they also don't want to date 40 people a month, right?

The Past Due Date on Product Packaging & Positioning

Everything has its day in the sun, and that includes your product angle. No matter how good it is, no matter how catchy and on target, one day it will be as stale as week old pizza. When it reaches this point, or preferably before, it is your job to determine if any of it can be saved, or if it needs to be completely discarded.

The longer you wait, the staler it gets. The staler it gets, the more repulsive it becomes. The more repulsive it becomes, the more repulsive YOU become.

Have we made our point? Go through your closet with a machete, cover your furniture with sheets if you have to, buy a few new cookbooks, and ask someone ten years younger than you what they say when something is really cool.

Sounds like work? Sounds like you've got to stay on your toes? Well, you do. The Dating Free Market is open all the time, and it's not for the tired or apathetic.

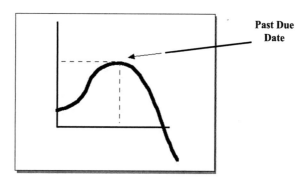

Don't Ignore Past Due Date on Product Packaging

55

ADVERTISING

"In our factory, we make lipstick. In our advertising,
we sell hope."
- Charles Revson

"Doing business without advertising is like winking at a girl in
the dark. You know what you are doing, but nobody else does."
- Steuart H. Britt

"The business that considers itself immune to the necessity
for advertising sooner or later finds itself immune to business."
- Derby Brown

Most people think advertising is very easy. In fact, most people think that advertising is for morons. Face it, after 40,000 hours of sitting in front of the television, even Ned the Beachcomber feels that he can make a better commercial than most of the ones he sees. To compound this impression we have a treasure-trove of era-defining jingles and slogans, such as:

- "Coke adds life"
- "It's always Coca Cola"
- "The Dot in Dot.com"
- "Don't Leave Home Without It"
- "Yo Quiero Taco Bell"
- "Are You Ready?"
- "Where's the Beef?"

Not exactly the work of Einstein, is it?

Or isn't it?

Advertising is hard work, and many of the best advertisers can be considered certifiable geniuses, if not at least simply certifiable. It is a skill that requires a profound understanding of the product, its benefits, the customers, their demographics and segmentation, their habits and likes, the ways they can be reached, how often they should be touched, what you should say and how to say it, how to get their attention, how to make them remember the ad, how to make them remember the company, how to make them remember the product, and how to make them remember what the product does. Plus, the slogan and jingle. We're talking nuclear physics here, because your fellow man and woman are not the simpletons that you believe.

According to the professors, advertising is:

...Activities that promote a product or business so as to make its existence publicly known and to draw attention and desire to specific qualities, resulting in an eventual purchase by a target market

This explanation is very crisp and academic. But just to make sure you get it, we will summarize the goal of advertising in dating as MTWI, which stands for:

"Make Them Want It"

Remember that you are the product. You have to get your customers to see it. You must tell them what they will experience if they get it. You must show them what it does and how they will benefit from it. You have to make them want it. You have to make them lust after it. They must have it. They must lust.

Shakespeare summed up lust fairly succinctly in Sonnet 129 when he wrote, "The expense of spirit in a waste of shame, is lust in action". The goal of your advertising, in addition to broadcasting your availability to your target market, is to create satisfiable lust. You have to make it palpable, make it become a need. Make it so great that they will do anything for it, for you, the product.

There are three basic themes for modern advertising, all based on the "experience" or "life events" that customers will enjoy. They are:

- **Sex**

- **Children**

- **Pets**

Sex in Advertising

Sex in advertising can be as subtle as an inkblot test ("Yes, I think I can see either the word 'Sex' or 'SFX' in a cloud of dust during the Lion King") or as blatant as Hooters ("Hooter, real big Hooters!")

Another way of putting it is, "What do women in bikinis have to do with motorcycles and monster trucks, and muscled shirtless men have to do with soft drinks?" The answer is nothing, they just catch your eye and enable the ephemeral but sufficient promise that based on your product choices sex is somewhere down the line.

Every business school has a course in which at some point sex in advertising is discussed. The classic example referenced is the Naked Woman in the Ice Cubes of a Drinking Glass photograph. Supposedly she's there, but the image is subliminal.

Sex in advertising is so widely used that it's practically a cliche. But then again, it works. It works in business, and it works in dating. A woman puts on a short, low-bustline dress with high-heels, and 9 out of 10 straight men are thinking "Sex!" Actually, what they are thinking when she walks by is the following:

•#1 - "What am I going to have for lunch? Eggs, a sandwich, a ... Sex!"

•#2 - "Man, how am I going to pay that bill ... Sex!"

•#3 - "That Joe is a pain in the ass, if he asks me again I'm going to ... Sex!"

•#4 - "My kids are really funny, why the other day Reggie said .... Sex!"

•#5 - "Jane wants me to pick up the laundry, do I have the stub ... Sex!"

•#6 - "I've got too much work to do today, I wonder if ... Sex!"

•#7 - "Wow look at her. No, look at that one. Uh-huh, look at this one ... Sex!"

•#8 - "Do I look important walking down the street? Maybe if I ... Sex!"

•#9 - "Sex! Sex! Sex!"

•#10 - "Damn dog pooh, can't someone clean up after them?"

This scenario is often repeated for some people when they see a muscular fellow in bike shorts. As you can see, sexy packaging and sex in advertising are closely linked, and often interchangeable.

Flirting

Flirting is another form of sex in advertising. What you are advertising is not only possible availability, but possible interest. One of the most attractive things you can indicate to a person is that you find them interesting (which is another reason to ask them about themselves). This point never changes in a relationship, you need to remain interested. Since flirting can be a bit ambiguous, what you're also advertising is mystery, which people find quite attractive as well.

The first step in flirting is simple - smile. Smiles are worth more than gold. Not only are they a barometer of good health, mental well-being, and ability to share, smiles are extremely sexy. Always smile when you flirt. Flirting without a smile is just idle banter. In fact, to flirt you often don't have to do anything but smile. There are three types of Flirting Smiles:

- Smile #1 - 'I find you interesting.'
- Smile #2 - 'I find you attractive.'
- Smile #3 - 'I find you humorous.'

Successful flirting is like squeezing a cantaloupe. Imagine you are at the supermarket and shopping for groceries, when you see a stall of ripe cantaloupe. You walk over, check them out, see one that catches your eye, and reach out and give it a little squeeze. You linger for a moment, then walk away and continue shopping. Ten minutes later you come back, see the cantaloupe still there, walk up, and give it another little squeeze. Nothing serious, you don't examine it for flaws or hold it up to the light. You just make sure that it looks comfortable - like it won't roll off of the cart - give it a little squeeze, linger a few moments, then go back to shopping. Ten minutes later you come back, see the cantaloupe is still there, and walk over again. This time however you want to make a bit more of an impression, so you squeeze it once, admire it for a few moments, then squeeze it again.

Get the point? When you flirt, you're not actually trying to complete an actual purchase transaction, you're just setting the stage for one. The fact is that after three good, evenly-spaced squeezes, this cantaloupe is more than ready to consider being bought. Every time you give it a squeeze - or in human talk, a brief friendly conversation or compliment - you are priming it for purchase. You are allowing it to have a good look at you, smiling of course, long enough to indicate your interest but short enough to be tantalizing.

If this cantaloupe analogy doesn't work for you then imagine yourself as a tray of delicious hors d'oeuvres carried around a party by a waiter that let's your prospect see but barely gets close enough for them to reach. Every time the waiter comes by, the prospect gets more and more interested. By the time they've finally reached the tray on its third round, they are a lot more interested than they would have been if the tray had just been laid on the table in front of them. Before they would have noticed, now they are interested.

Try "the cantaloupe method" the next time you see someone that you find attractive. Start with a smile and a "Hello," then walk away. Come back a few minutes later, look them in the eyes, and give them a little squeeze. Make conversation that shows you may be interested in them, preferably on a topic relating to what they are doing or the activities going on around you (party, park, bar, bat-mitzvah, christening, etc.). After five minutes excuse yourself and walk away.

Come back ten minutes later, smile, and converse on how you are doing with the activities taking place around you. Be positive, try to be humorous, be sure to ask how they are doing. After a while your prospect should start to appear much more ripe.

Touching

People like to be touched, but not often do they like to be mauled, especially by someone they don't really know. How can you do one without accomplishing the other? Go for the brief body contact. Brush hands, touch elbows, stand close enough together to rub shoulders. Remember that brief is key. Brief means that you don't stay in this position for more than two seconds, long enough for them to barely notice that you permeated their personal space without them being put on guard that you are there.

This is a hit-and-run flirting technique, and it really works. Just don't over do it, and keep it brief.

Don't forget another way to touch a person is by eye contact. Some people find eye contact, and eyes in general, to be quite erotic and intimate. Eye contact is essentially "rubbing eyes," which is something that you can only accomplish figuratively without injury. Eye contact is another way to get into personal space without invading personal space. It's usually brief enough not to frighten, and is a good indicator that you are actively listening to what a person is saying.

Children in Advertising

Children are another advertising gimmick. Throw a kid into a picture, it doesn't matter what, and people go all soft. "Oh, look at the baby! Look how well they're sitting next to the new tool box." Kids don't have to have anything to do with the product; advertisers just throw them in anyway. Really, they just toss them in because it seems like a child could fit in the shot. Why not, it works. The success of this ploy goes a long way in explaining how we keep getting subjected to really stupid movies where a fading adult actor teams up with. an irrepressible little tyke.

In the dating world, the kid angle is a double-edged sword. If you have kids, you already know how touchy the subject can be. Say the words, "I've got kids" and you may be seeing your date's backside a lot sooner than you expected, as they inch towards the door. On the other hand, it's better for you and the kids to separate the wheat from the chafe as early as possible. If you have kids and that scares your date, send the date on their way. They are not worth your hard-earned advertising resources.

Kids, however, are like honey to the bee when they aren't yours, especially if they're cute and young. The younger and cuter the better. If not cute, put them in a cute outfit, preferably with bunny rabbits. Many an uncle has taken his niece or nephew to the park or the mall simply to lure women into his personal space. "Oh, how cute. Are they yours" they ask. "No, I'm just the uncle" he says. "Well, they are so-o-o- cute" they reply, with implications that the uncle may produce cute children too and should be now considered a suitable dating prospect, especially since he doesn't appear to be afraid of kids.

Pets in Advertising

Pets are good advertising fodder as well. When pet food commercials come on the air, people stop and watch them, and most viewers don't even have pets. "Look at that dog. Oh look, he's talking. Oh, now he's running. Will he ever get that food before it dances away?"

Pets are like substitute children, except with fur. For this reason, we highly recommend incorporating them into your advertising strategy. It's very simple. Find a friend with a dog that doesn't bite and take them for a walk. The dog can be a bouncy puppy, a sturdy adult, or a creaking, flaking oldster, it doesn't matter. You take that dog out for one hour a day, at least twice a week, and you've got a new dating prospect every seven days. They just walk right up to you on the street and start talking.

"Can I pet him? He's such a nice dog. What a good, good doggy. What's his name?"

What's your name, baby?

In business, we call that "Opportunity knocking." In dating it's referred to as a "knocking opportunity."

With all of this insight on pets in advertising, you may say, "If one dog is good, more is better." You are right. More dogs are better for two reasons. First, there are more dogs for prospective dates to love. More questions to be asked, more small talk to be made. Second, by having more than one dog you have effectively created a pack, and instantiated yourself as its leader. Being leader of the pack is a major competitive advantage.

Negative Advertising

Whatever advertising strategy you use, try to deliver as much of the product as promised. At least, as much as promised based on your own sincere intentions, though those may not match your customer's perceptions. Be fair. Be smart. If you treat them shabbily, watch your ass. Customer dissatisfaction and negative word-of-mouth will sink you faster than the Titanic, and just as permanently.

My friend Jonah had this girlfriend that was absolutely in love with him in college. He was her first love, and she took him to see her parents, who absolutely fell in love with too. The whole family was into him. They seemed to figure that this man was the real thing, and you know, Jonah was this really great guy.

So Junior year Jonah goes to study in Germany, and his girlfriend Tina is back in school, waiting for him, because they've got a trip planned together for Christmas break. She's going to come over and visit him for two weeks, and she's got the tickets and everything ready to go.

But Jonah has started seeing Heidi, a girl from his school on the same study abroad trip, and they're starting to get into each other. But Tina is on her way, and Jonah doesn't say anything about Heidi to Tina until she steps off the plane. Then he just lowers the boom. He's like,"It's over" and all that.

She cries and is totally shocked. But they've got two weeks together in Europe, and it's going to be really weird. I don't know how, but they make it work and have a strained but alright time. So it seems like everything's cool, like she's cool with it.

But the next year I start running into girls from her college, because I'm up there occasionally, or I see them at some party in New York, you know. And I'm like, "Hey you went to blah, blah, do you know Tina?", and they go, "Yeah, we know her." Then I say, "Yeah, she used to go out with a friend of mine, Jonah." Then they go ice cold, man, totally ice cold. It's weird, because these are individual women. They're not together. This happens every time. They say, "You mean Jonah SMITH?"

This happens with about eight different women. It turns out that Tina went back and totally smeared Jonah around her entire campus. He's like a living legend now, but a bad one, like an "urban legend."

Negative word of mouth will kill you in dating.

Know Your Product

The key to advertising is knowing your product well; knowing what it really is. That makes it easier for you to come up with new and innovative ways to make people want it.

For example: You've got breasts? You like breasts? A lot of people have or like breasts too. But what are they really, besides fatty deposits, the ability to generate milk, and a reason to spend money on a bra?

According to Desmond Morris, author of The Naked Ape, human breasts mimic human buttocks. In the days before upright walking, standing, and face-to-face speaking, a woman's sexual readiness was communicated by the condition and color of her buttocks. Apparently we saw a lot of naked behinds back then, even more than we saw unshaven faces. Morris says that when humans began standing upright, and interacting less from behind and more from the front, we lost those sexual signals. This was a reproductive and evolutionary problem. We could stand, but we couldn't figure out when to have sex. So in order to recapture those signs, to make sure we didn't die out from shear stupidity, the human female's mammary glands began to swell, and in effect became in-your-face buttocks. The proof is that no other primate stands upright all of the time, or has these protruding mammary glands [breasts]. It's not a surprise then that when asked about the part of the body considered sexiest, most men saythe butt.

If you buy this explanation it gives you a pretty good idea of why many people react the way they do to cleavage. Check out the signage. Our point, know your product.

There is one basic, realistic objective of first-time advertising, and that is to make the customer aware of your product and its benefits. To reach that goal, you have to decide how you will utilize two key variables:

- Reach
- Frequency

These variables can be mixed in infinite combinations to get the desired results, but they need to be seriously considered when planning your advertising campaign.

Awareness

"Who the hell are you?"

Have you ever heard those words and thought, "One day they'll know who I am, and boy will they be sorry"? If you have, it's because the person you were talking to was not aware of the superior properties of your product. Awareness is critical, products don't sell themselves. Despite the belief of many an engineer and senior manager, if you build a better mousetrap the world will not beat a path to your door, they'll just say, "Hey, what do you guys do?"

There are different levels of awareness as well. There's familiarity, where someone sees a product and they say, "I think I've seen that person somewhere before," or, "Wasn't that the guy who tried to date you in high school and had a big zit coming out of his forehead?"

Another level is referred to as "top of mind" awareness. This is when a concept comes to your mind, and the product is the first thing you think of. Your friend says, "Isn't that a truck over there?", and you say, "Yeah, Doug has a truck." Or, your friend says, "I really like purses", and you say, "I saw this awesome woman over at Macy's the other day in the purse section. I think she works there."

Familiarity is OK. It may open the door to a conversation. Top of mind awareness, though, is your goal. It can do more than open the door for you, it can close it on your competitors.

Reach

You want to make your customers aware of you? Well, how do you reach them? Or more importantly, how far do you go to reach how many of them?

The term "reach"in advertising means just what says. "How far can you 'reach' your message into the market?" For example, let's say you're targeting Latin men. Do you broadcast an invitation to dinner on all of the radio stations on the air? If you do, then you have a very broad reach. Do you broadcast to all the stations that have Latin men as part of their demographics, but are not all Latin men? Perhaps, and this would be a much better use of your time and resources. Or, do you broadcast at 7pm on the drive home from work on the station with the Latin men talk show? Definitely.

As you can see, you can have a broad reach, or a narrow reach. It depends on the size, composition, and availability of your market. Have you noticed how at 3 am in the morning Phone Sex commercials come on every television station still broadcasting? It's because they have the greatest chance of reaching a large number of people with nothing to do but sit around alone and watch television with no one to talk to. Plus, everyone's asleep and no one is going to hear them (and phone rates are definitely cheaper at night, aren't they?). If these commercials were broadcast during the day they might reach more possible customers, but the ratio of qualified prospects would be much lower and therefore the costs would be a lot higher.

The health club is the most obvious place for advertising. Granted, some people go there to stay in shape, or to get in shape, but why are they doing this? In order to live longer? In order to feel better? Because their friends do it? There are many good reasons, and if you say them enough times you actually start believing them. It doesn't matter why you started going to the gym, what matters is the reason why you keep going back: the advertisements. "Look at me, I'm really strong." "Look at me, I can run a long time." "Look at me, I'm losing weight." "Look at me, I've got a new outfit on, and check out my sneakers." Talk about subliminal.

The one thing that is worse than bad advertising is a chance to advertise and not doing so. If you're going to go to the gym, at least keep in mind that someone there is looking at you, and they may or may not see someone that they like - you. You shouldn't think about this while you're working out, but you definitely should think about it when you pack that gym bag... and look for a spotter... and decide what are the best hours and days of the week to go... and stand in the big mirrors that make you look really hot and sexy. Don't forget to bring a pen and paper.

So ask yourself, how do you reach your target?

Someone once asked Jesse James (or some equally well-known bandit), "Why do you rob banks?", to which he replied, "Because that's where the money is."

Are you advertising "where the money is"?

Frequency

Frequency is another important part of the advertising mix. It focuses on how often you repeat the advertisement for your audience. You have to determine if you're going to play it once a week, once a day, twice a day, twice an hour, etc. Repetition is very important in driving top-of-mind awareness, especially in the initial phases of a campaign. Every jingle and slogan that you've ever quoted has come at the price of repeated hammering through your eardrums and into your brain cells, stamped in eternal aural graffiti on your cerebrum.

Too little frequency is a waste of effort. So you showed up at one party last year. Do you really think that this was enough? Only if you're Cinderella. If you want to make an impression, you've got to get out and about. See and be seen.

On the other hand, you don't want to be seen too much. If you attend every function in your market, shoveling your "I'm available and here's what we have to offer" advertisement over and over down your customers' throats, then they will eventually suffer from "over saturation." Over-saturation is the death knell of advertising. It means that people are basically sick of it. They've had enough, they're bored, and they tune out. All your future efforts are thus wasted, or at best, pathetic.

For these reasons, you must treat your frequency as a science. Too little and only a handful of people will remember your name, too much and they won't want to hear it again.

Online Banner Advertising = T-Shirts

T-shirts as a means of advertising your product are about as effective as online banner advertising was in 1999. Back then, all the Internet gurus extolling the benefits of the New Economy and the Death of the Old Media claimed that online advertising was the wave of the future. Little advertising banners, or micro billboards, were plastered on websites of all sizes and shapes. Purchasing companies were charged based on the number of "views" (the number of people who came to the website and therefore "saw" the ad) or by the number of click-throughs (the number of times people clicked on the ad, taking them to your product's website).

Banner advertising was extremely popular at this time. Part of their appeal was that an advertiser could more effectively target potential customers based on the type of website they visited. If your target market segment was known to like Italian cooking and travel, you placed an ad on ladolcevita.com. If your market was into dogs, Pets.com might be your place (if they sold ad space). Companies literally fought each other to throw their money at websites for banner ad space, sometimes contracting out as far as a year in advance for fear of not getting room on it later. Fees went up, up, up, and the revenues of dot-coms like Yahoo, Spycast, and DoubleClick went soaring as well. Then in 2000 a little problem began creeping out of the woodwork. Click throughs were down, and sales based on banner driven website traffic were down too. The problem was that the market was oversaturated. People were getting used to seeing so many ads that they basically started to ignore most of them. If a merchant tried to counteract that effect with a really flashy banner ad then that was perceived as negative as well because it was too distracting for users. To make things worse, studies started appearing which questioned if banner ads ever really were effective, or at least any more effective than an ordinary print ad or a highway billboard.

The only true exception to this ad downturn was the adult-oriented Internet market, where banner ads promising "Live Nude Do-It-All Barely Legal Babes" or "Big Strong Strapping Stripping Not-Straight-At-All Men" were the primary means of driving customer traffic from one site the other. Men, most of the customers, forever looking for the next best thing went from site to site, checking out thousands of dirty pictures and clicking on banner after banner. The adult Internet market essentially consisted of a giant web of sites linked to each other by hundreds of racy banners. In this market niche, banner ad effectiveness was proven by the high level of profitability enjoyed by Internet porn startups.

Needless to say, with the exception of the porn market, banner ad fees dropped like a dead monkey falling out of a tree. Things became so desperate that some vendors even gave away large amounts of ad space, so as to entice you to sign at least some kind of deal.

T-shirts as a way to advertise your product are about as effective as online banner ads were. Essentially you are putting a product statement on your chest, and hoping that after a certain amount of "views" you'll hit the right customer who will want to click-through. Unfortunately, unless your offer is of the adult nature and you've got the goods to back it up, your response rate is going to be about the same as some of those many defunct dot-coms.

Top 15 T-Shirt Slogans
(and why they work as well as online banner advertising unless you're under age 17)

- (Big Arrow pointing towards your crotch)
- I Love NY
- Metallica
- Girls Rule
- [X] have more fun!
- I'm with Stupid
- Gap
- Kiss me, I'm Horny
- Kiss me, I'm Irish
- Kiss me, I'm Italian
- Kiss me, I'm Polish
- I Love LA
- Phat Farm
- Harvard
- Plumbers Lay More Pipe

Top 15 T-Shirt Slogans That Many Men Wish They Could See on Women

- Ask Me My Name and I'll Sleep With You
- You Are So Hot
- Buy Me A Drink and I'll Sleep With You
- Girls Rule, and Two Girls Rule Twice as Long
- Check Out My T-Shirt, Especially the Parts that Are on My Nipples
- I'm with Stupid, but I'll Dump Them for You Baby
- Kiss me, I'm Horny
- Kiss me, I'm Irish
- Kiss me, I'm Italian
- Kiss me, I'm Polish
- Kiss me, I'm Hot
- Orgy Town
- I Want to Be Your Sex Slave
- I'll Pay for Everything
- You May Be My Soul Mate

Top 15 T-Shirt Slogans That Many Women Wish They Could See on Men

- Ask Me My Name and I'll Marry You
- You Are So Hot
- Buy Me A Drink and I'll Take You to France
- Girls Rule, and Two Girls Are Twice as Smart as Ten Men
- My Other T-Shirt is a Suit
- I'm Funny, Nice, and a Good Cook
- I'm with Stupid, She's Definitely Not as Nice as You
- Kiss me, I'm Horny
- Kiss me, I'm Irish
- Kiss me, I'm Italian
- Kiss me, I'm Polish
- I Want to Be Your Domestic Servant
- I'll Pay for Everything
- Can You Spell, R-E-L-A-T-I-O-N-S-H-I-P
- I've Got a Gallon of Peach Ice Cream at Home

Print Advertising

Date advertising can utilize several non-traditional vehicles. These include basketballs, offices, trains, swimming pools, night clubs, and street corners. With these vehicles your imagination is your strongest ally. But in traditional media such as print, imagination and clarity are even stronger. The Classified, or Personal, Ads are perfect examples. The Classifieds are a powerful and economical method to reach a mass audience.

You can use a Classified Ad in several ways. You can use it to educate. You can use it to inform. You can use it to entice and persuade. You can even use it to promote special deals (e.g. two for ones). You just have to make sure that you are clear in your messaging.

Ask yourself these questions: What are we really saying in the Personal ads? What hidden messages, attitudes, and product flaws and features are we communicating? How do we stand out from the crowd? Finally, are we attracting our target market, or just marketing our targets?

To illustrate how to answer these questions, let's take a look at seven sample Classified Ads.

SAMPLE CLASSIFIED ADS
(MEN SEEKING WOMEN, WOMEN SEEKING MEN)

I'm 28 yrs. old, 5'9" tall with an athletic build, long brown hair & medium brown eyes. I'm looking for someone taller than me with a nice build. Someone older than me but not too old. Someone with a good sense of humor, a nice personality & definitely housebroken.

Your wisdom & spirituality balance your keen intellect. You're mature & sensitive yet strong & not swayed by popular opinion because you perceive a deeper truth. You seek a woman who's more inclined towards mysticisms than politics. Your sole purpose for being on this line is to find love & increase good feelings in your life. Be between 35-43 yrs. of age. I'm a 38 yr. old brunette with long, wavy hair, 5'4" tall & weigh 130 lbs.

I'm a single, black female who's searching for a special lover who can help me rediscover my sensual, seductive persona. I'm 43 yrs. old, 5'7", 138 lbs. with an athletic build, medium brown skin, dark brown eyes & short brown/black hair. I seek a man who enjoys long, deep & passionate kisses that caress the lips & set the mouth on fire. Someone who enjoys being explored until he tingles. Do you love the idea of being seduced, pampered & surprised? Are you seeking one lover & one lover only? If you're 5'10" or taller with an athletic build, handsome & have a wild, adventurous nature, then you & I may have something to talk about.

I'm a 5'10", 165 lb. fit, lean, attractive, single male with a very fine body. I'm interested in talking & meeting for a possible intimate encounter & maybe more with someone who doesn't limit themselves by age. Someone who's a non-smoker, doesn't wear a lot of make-up & looks great in shorter skirts. I'm very sensual, drive & have a high libido. I'm very affection & love pleasing whoever I'm with. If interested in a great lover, please leave a message.

Long term investment with daily profits. SWM, 50s ISO single, petite female. I'm giving, sexy and ready.

Beautiful man seeking beautiful, depressed woman. If you or someone you know fits this description, know that there is one other.

Hunchback with lazy eye, cleft palate seeks kindly nurse to change drool cup

Now, let's look at our Marketing Analysis of the same Classified Ads (OUR COMMENTS CAPITALIZED AND IN BOLD FONT):

#1

- I'm 28 yrs. old, 5'9" tall with an athletic build, long brown hair & medium brown eyes **LONG BROWN HAIR IS CONSIDERED SEXY, BUT WHAT THE HECK ARE "MEDIUM BROWN" EYES?.** I'm looking for someone taller than me with a nice build. **SHE SHOULD JUST SAY "I NEED SOMEONE TO LOOK UP TO"** Someone older than me but not too old. **"NO ONE OUT OF MY DEMOGRAPHICS - GENERATION X"** Someone with a good sense of humor, a nice personality **AMBIGUOUS AND OPEN-ENDED! WHO REALLY THINKS THAT THEY'RE AN ASSHOLE?** & definitely housebroken **WHAT DOES THAT MEAN? THEY AREN'T A SLOB, OR THAT THEY CAN COOK?.**

  OUR EVALUATION: DEAR, YOU ARE ALL OVER THE MAP. WHAT DO YOU WANT AGAIN, BESIDES SOMEONE JUST LIKE YOU? EVER THOUGHT OF CLONING?

#2

- I'm a single, black female **ISN'T THAT WHAT "SBF" STANDS FOR, SHE'S GETTING KIND OF WORDY. MAYBE SHE'S A MOTOR MOUTH. MAYBE SHE DOESN'T WANT ANY MISUNDERSTAND-INGS, CLARITY IS IMPORTANT** who's searching for a special lover who can help me rediscover my sensual, seductive persona **BECAUSE I'VE BEEN WITHOUT SEX FOR SO LONG THAT I'VE FORGOT-TEN WHAT IT IS LIKE.** I'm 43 yrs. old, 5'7", 138 lbs. with an athletic build **ALL THESE NUMBERS ARE FORCING ME TO DO MATH AND FIGURE OUT IF SHE REALLY IS ATHLETICALLY BUILT. IN MATH THEY CALL THIS A "PROOF"** , medium brown skin, dark brown eyes & short brown/black hair **ALL AFRICAN-AMERICANS AREN'T MADE ALIKE, BUT DIDN'T SHE ALREADY SAY SHE WAS BLACK? I'M ASSUMING SHE HAS BROWN SKIN AND BROWN EYES AND BROWN HAIR. I ONLY NEED TO KNOW IF THAT IS *NOT* THE CASE. BLAH, BLAH, BLAH....** I seek a man who enjoys long, deep & passionate kisses that caress the lips & set the mouth on fire **WHEW! SOMEONE GET A FIRE EXTINGUISHER, THIS LADY IS H-O-R-N-Y!.** Someone who enjoys being explored until he tingles **THAT'S THE DEAL-CLOSER RIGHT THERE. YOU GO**

GIRL!. Do you love the idea of being seduced, pampered & surprised? **ACTUALLY, I LOVE THE IDEA BUT NOT EVERY DAY, IF THAT'S WHAT SHE'S GOT IN MIND. CAN'T WE JUST CUDDLE?** Are you seeking one lover & one lover only **"NO PLAYERS, PLEASE" YEAH. RIGHT. WHO ELSE IS GOING TO ANSWER THIS AD?** If you're 5'10" or taller with an athletic build, handsome **YEAH BABY, I THINK I'M VERY HANDSOME (THOUGH EVERYONE DOESN'T AGREE WITH ME, BUT SCREW THEM)** & have a wild, adventurous nature **ARE WE TALKING "9 1/2 WEEKS" WILD, OR "BODY HEAT" WILD?** , then you & I may have something to talk about. **OK, WHEN DID TALKING ENTER THE PICTURE?**

OUR EVALUATION: SHE'S SO UNDERSEXED THAT SHE'LL WRITE ANYTHING TO GET IT. UNFORTUNATELY, SHE'LL ALSO GET ANYTHING BUT WHAT SHE'S LOOKING FOR WHEN GUYS RESPOND

#3

Long term investment with daily profits. SWM, 50s ISO single, petite female. I'm giving, sexy and ready. **OHH, HE'S SPEAKING THE FINANCIAL LINGO OF THE WELL-OFF! OR THE PSEUDO WELL-OFF, WHO CAN TELL? MONEY TALKS, AND MY MONEY TALKS ABOUT MY VIEW OF THE WORLD. EITHER WAY, HE'S SAYING "ONLY TINY LITTLE TROPHY WIVES SHOULD APPLY"**

OUR EVALUATION: GOLDDIGGERS ARE SHARPENING THEIR KNIVES AS THEY READ THIS, THINKING "ANOTHER SUCKER"

#4

- Your wisdom & spirituality balance your keen intellect **OK, SHE'S ALREADY ELIMINATED PEOPLE WHO DON'T READ A LOT.** You're mature & sensitive yet strong & not swayed by popular opinion because you perceive a deeper truth **I WAS WITH YOU UNTIL THE "BECAUSE" PART. I'M GOING TO HAVE TO READ THAT ALL OVER AGAIN AND SEE IF I FIT. WAIT A MINUTE, THIS IS ALREADY TOO MUCH WORK.** You seek a woman who's more inclined towards mysticisms than politics **SO ARE WE TALKING SEX WITH CRYSTALS AND CANDLES HERE?**. Your sole purpose for being on this line is to find love & increase good feelings in your life

BEING ON WHAT LINE? IF I HAVE TO ASK THIS QUESTION THEN I GUESS I'M NOT ON IT. Be between 35-43 yrs. of age. I'm a 38 yr. old brunette with long, wavy hair, 5'4" tall & weigh 130 lbs. IS THAT THE RIGHT WEIGHT FOR 5'4"? AND DOES WAVY HAIR REALLY MEAN FRIZZY HAIR?

OUR EVALUATION: WE'RE THINKING BIRKENSTOCKS RIGHT ABOUT NOW, BUT WE WISH HER LUCK FINDING SOMEONE ON THE SAME "LINE"

#5

- I'm a 5'10", 165 lb. fit, lean, attractive, single male with a very fine body MODESTY, SCHMODESTY, TELL 'EM LIKE IT IS. I'm interested in talking & meeting for a possible intimate encounter READ BETWEEN THE LINES, "I'M NOT PRESSURING YOU IF YOU SHOW UP TO JUMP INTO BED WITH ME...IMMEDIATELY" & maybe more SO MAYBE IT'S NOT ALL ABOUT SEX...MAYBE with someone who doesn't limit themselves by age I'M MUCH OLDER THAN YOU ARE. Someone who's a non-smoker, doesn't wear a lot of make-up IN THIS DAY AND AGE NOT MANY PEOPLE DO UNLESS THEY'RE OLD! HA! YOU'VE GIVEN YOURSELF AWAY, YOU'RE SOME OLD GUY LOOKING FOR A HOT YOUNG FREAKY CHICK & looks great in shorter skirts YUP, THERE YOU GO! AND HE'S NOT SEXIST EITHER, JUST "SEXUAL" I'm very sensual, drive & have a high libido "I'M A HORNY OLD GUY AND AM HORNY ALL THE TIME. BE READY FOR SOME GOOD LOVIN', WOMAN". I'm very affection & love pleasing whoever I'm with "SEE, I'M SENSITIVE AND INTO THIS NEW AGE, PLEASE-THE-WOMAN STUFF" [WE'RE ASSUMING "WHOEVER" APPLIES TO A WOMAN, BUT MAYBE NOT]. If interested in a great lover "BECAUSE SOMEONE ONCE TOLD ME THAT I WAS AND I BELIEVED IT. BE PREPARED TO AGREE WITH THIS ASSESSMENT, WHETHER YOU LIKE IT OR NOT", please leave a message. "OR SEND ME YOUR USED PANTIES, YEAH!"

OUR EVALUATION: HE'S GOT A GOOD BODY FOR SOMEONE HIS AGE AND WANTS TO CONTINUE TO USE IT SEXUALLY. BUT...DON'T EXPECT THAT HE DOESN'T LOOK LIKE A PERVERT, OR THAT HE LOOKS LIKE SOME SWINGIN' STUD

#6

- Beautiful man seeking beautiful, depressed woman. If you or someone you know fits this description, know that there is one other. **ALRIGHTY THEN, IF HE'S SO GOSH-DARNED BEAUTIFUL THEN WHY IS HE PREYING ON THE EMOTIONALLY VULNERABLE?**

  OUR EVALUATION: RUN! RUN FAST! RUN LIKE THE WIND! RUN AND DON'T TURN BACK!

#7

- Hunchback with lazy eye, cleft palate seeks kindly nurse to change drool cup **IS HE KIDDING OR SERIOUS? IF HE'S SERIOUS THEN HE'S LOOKING FOR A HUNCHBACK LOVER, WHICH APPARENTLY THERE ARE ENOUGH OF TO JUSTIFY THIS AD. YOU KNOW, HUNCHBACKS NEED LOVE TOO. MAYBE HE REALLY DOESN'T HAVE A HUNCHBACK, BUT DOES HAVE A LAZY EYE? OOHH, THIS IS SO MYSTERIOUS, I MUST CALL!**

  OUR EVALUATION: IF HE'S NOT SEROUS THEN THIS GUY IS A TOTAL IDIOT, AND KIND OF INSENSITIVE, JUST WHAT A MODERN WOMAN WANTS

As you can see, writing the best marketing copy for a classified ad isn't easy. Obviously these people did not use any of the proven business school lessons before launching this marketing vehicle.

Let's try them again. First, we'll rewrite each Classified Ad using the "Truth in Advertising" adage, which is very popular with consumer advocate groups, but doesn't sell a lot of dates. Afterwards, we'll re-create the ads using product messaging and positioning.

"TRUTH IN ADVERTISING" CLASSIFIEDS

#1

I'm a 28 yrs. old SWF and I like to work out a lot, so my body is in pretty good shape. I value this, so I only want men who are also in pretty good shape. My face is pretty average, but I have nice long brown hair that is not too common, and you may be into long hair. My eyes are brown, but if you look really close you'll see they're not black. Since high school I've only dated taller men, so I'm not changing that requirement until I'm desperate, which I'm not quite just yet. Men my age are not interested in me because they're still young enough to go for superficial things like good looks, so I figure an older guy would be more mature about this type of thing, maybe even ready to settle down (which is why he can't be a slob, because he may end up living with me). Of course, if he's not within five years of my age then his body won't be in the same good shape as mine, and we won't share the same sense of humor, so there you go. Anyone interested?

#2

I'm a SBF and I haven't had really good sex in a long, long, long time. I'm not dead yet (I'm only 43), so I'm not ready to give up on sex, and am willing to place this ad hoping that a decent man with lust in his heart comes along. I'm average height for a woman, though I'm not as skinny as Halle or Kate, but I look like I work out and you'll probably like it. As I've said, I'm African American, so I've got the lovely brown skin, eyes, and hair that you'd expect and love. It's been a long time since I've even kissed anyone like I did in high school, so be ready to French like it is going out of style. I mean "slob-city." Tongues and lips everywhere! Come on up for breath! Plus, I can use my hands in ways that would make you think you had a full-body sex massage, and am ready to put them to work. Listen up, though. I'm not interested in someone who's playing the field. If you want all of these sexual goodies then you've got to commit. I'm tired of sharing men with other women, and not having a date on Saturday night. And, I might as well say that you have to be over 5'10", well-built, and ready to get freaky. Don't be shocked, I'm no Vanessa Williams, but I'll rock your world!

#3

I'm a SWM in my 50's. I've got some money set aside for retirement, and made a little in the stock market. I'm ready for a serious long-term relationship, though I'm not saying if I've had any previously, and how they ended. Age isn't important, race isn't important (I think). She just has to be small, though I'm not going to say why because you'll have to meet me first and then you'll understand. Did I mention that I'm sexy? Well I am, so that means that I could want to have sex, not just coffee. Did I mention that I have a little money to play with? I could be a Sugar Daddy if you play your cards right. And you know that my use of the word "petite" implies that you know what it means, and therefore you are cultured? OK, I'm waiting, and I'm not getting any younger.

#4

I'm a woman. A very deep, spiritual, poetic, free-thinking, mystical woman. These are what make me who I am. I am not changing, and shouldn't have to. There are men like myself, and I invite them to join me at the metaphysical level, bringing positive vibes into the world. Can you dig it? Looks shouldn't matter, so all I can tell you is that I have brown hair, am not too tall, and not to heavy or thin. If you can't understand what I'm saying here, and it doesn't turn you on, then you're just like the other pathetic sheep out there.

#5

I'm a MAN, baby! Average height, lower than average weight, and it looks good on me. I know because I check the mirror every five minutes. Guys my age have all gone to pot, but me, I still look GOOD! I am no longer interested in those flabby women of my generation. I want a little Generation X, as in seX! Short skirts, tight pants, all ready to come off when I want them to, because my first and foremost priority is seX, seX, seX! I am very horny. Please help me. I'm going a little nuts looking at all of these younger women. At my age, I really don't need another relationship, I just need to know I can still "get some". I'm taking a shot and hoping that this ad works, and gets me some freaky-deaky chicks!

#6

I think that I am one hot dude, and people agree. I usually can pretend to be sensitive long enough to get what I want, so I like to focus on cute chicks that are depressed or lonely, then dazzle them with my looks and emotions. Then I screw them, and move on. If you are desperate enough to respond to this ad, or just have the poor judgement that has gotten you into similar situations, then you're the one for me.

I'm no Brad Pitt. I'm kind of strange [looking?]. But I have a unique
sense of humor. And this was the best I could think of, so here you
go. "I loved the Humpback of Notre Dame!" Quasimodo was so
unjustly treated. If you feel the same way, then you feel like me.
I AM Quasimodo. Now that you've said you're sympathetic to our
plight, call me, don't be a hypocrite.

OK, see what a rigid "Truth in Advertising" policy gets you when you're
looking for a date? Not a lot, except for sympathy. A businessperson who releases
a product with all of its features and flaws plainly exposed to the public is not
going to be employed for very long. The truth is that you cannot just present the
product and allow the market to draw its own conclusions. You have to lead them
to the conclusion that you want them to have, which is primarily that they must
have it.

With this in mind, let's apply our market research, our competitive advantage, and our packaging & positioning to the Classifieds, and show you how they
should really look:

THE BUSINESS SCHOOL CLASSIFIEDS

#1

Body like a triathelete! Seeks same in a man who can see the
horizon, loves to run his fingers through my long chestnut mane, and
is mature enough to appreciate the delights of a 28 yrs old young
woman. If he keeps his place clean enough, can laugh out loud, and
can treat me the way I'll treat him, I might just stay the night.

#2

I'm a Daughter of the Sun, a Woman of Color, with a great firm body.
Brown, beautiful, luscious is what I am, from the top of my head
down to my.... If you're lucky, loyal, and in good enough shape to
meet my "physical" needs, then you will be the fortunate one who
can enjoy all of the pleasures and skills that I have acquired in 43
years. And they are many! To take me in your arms and look down
into my eyes you have to be over 5'10", but that's it for the minimum
requirements. Do I make you Horny?

#3

I'm a man of means in my 50's, and I've discovered two things recently. The first is that I'd like to meet a petite woman who can help me enjoy my money over the long term. The second is that women find me very, very sexy. I guess the best things in life come with experience. Are you ready to benefit from mine?

#4

You're a man of the world, the metaphysical world. You see things others don't see, you know things that others don't know. You have evolved, advanced, beyond the material and superficial to a level that is almost tantric. That's where you'll meet me. You'll know me when you see me, my long wavy brown hair blowing in the cosmic wind. Shouldn't you have the soul mate that you deserve?

#5

I can go all night. That may frighten you a bit, but think of the possibilities. Imagine wearing that short skirt hanging in your closet for just the right occasion. I AM that right occasion. No makeup required, just a healthy libido.

#6

My external beauty is matched only by my sensitivity to your feelings. You are hurt, you are depressed, and yet you are beautiful too. We should be together. Let the healing begin. I will be your support, you will be my muse. Life is for the living..

#7

"I loved the Humpback of Notre Dame!" because it exposed the decayed values of those seeking wealth and external beauty. You loved it because you are educated, sympathetic, and progressive. You know that there is more to life than good looks. You can hear words that are left unspoken. You are special. So am I. We deserve each other. Call me, and let's discuss. Or meet me at the belltower.

Look at all that gloss! But see the difference? Instead of describing what the seller wants, or all of the long boring details of their lives, we talk about product benefits like how they will make you feel, how they will change your life, what they say about you as a savvy consumer. Instead of describing an empty cardboard box as an empty cardboard box, we call it a "lightweight, collapsible, personal storage unit for those that plan ahead."

Yeah man, I want one of those!

Long live advertising!

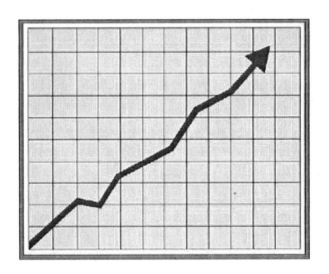

FINANCES AND PROMOTIONS

You've got the customers, but now how are you going to pay for the dating endeavor? How should you spend your money and resources? How do you keep the flow of prospects coming when competition is high? The answers to these questions are based in Financial theory and Sales Promotions.

To start, you should know that a basic principle of finance is that assets generate income, and liabilities produce expenses. In other words, if someone is "kind of just there" or "kind of alright" and the two of you are in a non-productive relationship, this is not an asset. It may not be a liability, but it is not an asset. An asset produces a benefit. "Just kind of there" is not a benefit.

Your goal is not only to finance your love life, but to treat the bottom line as you would a business. You want high-value assets. That is, you want emotional revenue and physical income.

The Cost/Benefit Analysis

Relationships are like businesses in more ways than one. When trying to decide if we're going to do something, we often forget to understand if we "should" do something. Should I ask this person out again? Should I invest in this power plant? Should I give them a birthday gift? Should I close down that department?

Businesses resemble us because they are composed of us. We run them, we work for them. They are an extension of human society.

When a company is young, decisions are made quickly, and often without a lot of deep thought. Time is of the essence, and we go with our gut feelings and emotions. We don't have a lot of experience, but we jump right in and say, "Yeeehaaaaa! Let's do this thing! I know that this is the way to go!"

When we're a little older and more seasoned, we slow down our decision making based on exuberance, and go more on our experiences, "Nope. Not interested. I dealt with a firm like that before and I got burned. Sorry, that's how we do things around here. You'll understand one day."

This is exactly how we are in personal relationships. When we're younger we rush in with our hearts, and when we're older we think we're being more intellectual and logical, even though our decisions are based on emotions created by past experiences. We think a lot, but the thoughts are all driven by feelings, not analysis.

As we mature we "think" that we have the benefit of experience on our side. This hypothesis may not be true. We may actually have emotional baggage on our side created from experience. This baggage is good if it keeps us out of the hands of a serial moocher and liar, but it's bad if it makes us continually dismiss new prospects.

There is a theory in finance called The Random Walk Theory. The Random Walk Theory statistically addresses the ability to predict the movement of a stock or the stock market based on past experience. Essentially, the Random Walk Theory says you can't. Forget the hype, most people will never see the promised returns of this kind of "savvy" investing. Despite what many Brokers say to the contrary, with few exceptions [i.e. the CEO's a junkie, the factory is out of parts, the SEC is going to split them up] it cannot be done. We repeat: You Can't Predict the Present Based on Past Experience. Remember this, because it's often true of dates as well.

Dating & relationships have a distinctive edge over businesses in the area of experience. In dating, sometimes the "Yeeeehaaaa!" approach is much more satisfying in the long-run, even if it is flawed. When was the last time that you met someone new and went "Yeeeehaaaa"? Do you think it's the quality of people? It isn't. It's your attitude. You can't "Yeeeehaaaa!" Forget your age, you should re-learn how to go "Yeeeehaaaa!". "They aren't perfect, they aren't a 10, they don't match my dreams, this may not end in marriage, but Yeeeehaaaa!" "Yeeeehaaaa!" is truly the meaning of 'feeling young at heart.'

Keep an open mind. The first date that didn't look too promising might end up being a lot more pleasant than cleaning your broom closet, or vice versa. They may actually produce positive revenue. Look at the real costs and real possible benefits, and then decide if it's worth your time.

Types of Costs

Rational objectivity is why companies like to hire MBAs. They are educated to stay objective about costs. MBAs come in and the first thing they say is, "Why should we do this? Let's do a Cost/Benefit Analysis."

A Cost/Benefit analysis means exactly what it says. You look at every major decision or operation, and decide if the costs outweigh the benefits.

There are several types of costs to examine. There are:

Financial Costs

"How much is this? Do we have the money? How much will it cost me in dollars and cents?"

Opportunity Costs

"What could I be doing instead of this? If I do this, will I miss out on something better?"

Strategic Costs

"I can only do 2 out of 3 important activities. Which are going to get me closer to my objectives?"

Plus, we are inventing a new cost, specifically for dating. We're going to call it, the Experience/Emotional Cost.

Experience/Emotional Costs

"Will I gain new experience from this? Will it help me, do nothing either way, or will I be scarred for life?"

Having defined the costs, one then looks at the benefits. If the costs as defined all outweigh the benefits, then you should not go forward. But if they don't, that in itself is a compelling reason to consider moving in a positive direction.

Puritan ideals are not necessarily in synch with business goals. On one side we say, "Look before you leap, " and "Sin in haste, repent at leisure," and on the other we say, "No pain, no gain," and "An opportunity missed is an opportunity lost." Your romantic goal is to not miss any possible opportunities, while balancing the costs.

Money Equals Power, But Not Vice Versa

Another financial principle you need to know is the contradiction that the impact of Power is greater than the impact of Money, but Money equals Power.

The Golden Rule says that she who has the gold makes the rules. Gold is just one form of currency among many, yet whoever is holding a large amount of it is in charge. This is true of all valuable currencies, and doesn't matter if you are a Venture Capitalist, a Banker, a Bus Driver, or a Poet. You must recognize the Balance of Power before you can use it or change it.

Paying for a date is a form of respect and politeness. It is a tribute to your guest. At this time they are the ones in power. "Are they pleased? Are they happy?" are the questions that keep you on your toes. Paying for a vacation is another exercise in power - the payer's. "Am I indebted? Am I happy? Am I going to get sent back if I'm annoying?" are the questions that keep the guest on their toes.

Remember the Golden Rule. It is advisable that in dating as in life, we try to keep some amount of monetary control of the situation.

Investment Vehicles

One way of getting control of your love life is by being able to comfortably afford it. There are several ways that this can be accomplished. You have a number of investment vehicles from which to choose:

Funding Choice	Use for Dating Pool
Savings	No
Checking	Yes
Stocks	No
Bonds	Yes
Credit Cards	Maybe

Savings Account

Use your savings account? Get real! Your Savings are for you and your future, don't touch them just to go on a date. That's just pathetic.

Checking Account

If you have any money left after paying your bills, buying food and clothing, and putting a little in savings, what's left is your basic dating fund. If you can't go on dates with what you have, get creative and find less expensive ways to have a good date. Museums, small bars with live music, bookstores, high school football games, college track meets, cafes, auto shows, dog walking, going to the park, playing volleyball and Frisbee, the spectators' sidewalk of a long-distance marathon, are all low cost ways to have a good time and not go broke. Remember, your money is not the only currency that you possess (see, Competitive Advantage).

Stocks and Options

Though stocks have been known to line many a geek's coffers, they are essentially too unpredictable to use as a source of funding for dating. Stocks are volatile, and your dating life could be as equally volatile if you tie it to your stock portfolio. Even more dangerous, your ego and self confidence will be as overinflated or undervalued as your investments.

Bonds

Bonds are a good bet if set up well in advance. Bonds produce an ongoing stream of income that never varies. For example, a 10% bond will provide you with a monthly payment of the same amount all year long. You can count on it being there, even if your stocks are down and your checking account is low. With bonds you will always have dating cash flow. (Caution: beware of dates that are highly leveraged by junk bonds)

Credit Cards

Credit cards are not really an investment vehicle. They can be used as a source of funds, but they essentially create more debt. Only if you stick with cards whose balances you must pay off at the end of the month, like American Express or Diners Club, or you have the self-discipline to them pay off , should you rely on credit to get you through a date. There is a serious downside to relying on credit cards. If you fail to pay off the balances because they are too high due to your exuberance, desire to impress, or extreme generosity, then you've created a problem that will make it harder for you to have the peace of mind needed to actually be in control and therefore a good date. In fact, over time your worry and weakening finances will eventually have you acting like a "cheap date," as you constantly calculate prices in your head.

That's right, we can see you doing it, and it is not attractive.

Investment Tip #1 - "Buy Low, Sell High"

Discount Sales = Stock up on Dating Essentials Now

Rationale:
Why wait until you're on a date to have the tools that you will need to keep it moving forward? Necessities such as mints, chewing gum, extra toothbrushes, condoms, creams, and spare socks can be purchased in advance of anyone actually using them. Stash them in easy to get to places for before, during, or after your date. Gift items for Holidays, Valentines Day, 3rd Dates, or Birthdays should also be inventoried. Perfect candidates include ties, inexpensive jewelry, cards, etc. If you can buy Starbuck's gift certificates at a discount, get them now. You will need as many as possible to keep "treating" dates to an extra cup of java.

One ongoing discount sale is the prix fixe dinner. Prix fixe meals, where you get delicious two, three, or four course dinners at a set price (excluding drinks) are one of Western Civilization's great bargains. The restaurants are usually quite nice, and the food is often quite good. This is the perfect opportunity to make your money work for you. Before your dates, scout out all of the restaurants in town that offer prix fixe meals. Start with French and Italian, of course. Then investigate the fusion spots, Californian-Jamaican, Hanoi-Swedish, New York-Buloxi. Don't forget the hotels, which are often prix fixe jackpots. Once you have identified the restaurants, their prices, their menus, and the days and times for prix fixe, you can set yourself a budget that allows you to be culinarily daring while staying fiscally conservative. You can go ahead and build yourself a nice "gourmet" reputation.

Investment Tip #2

Promote Customer Loyalty: Buy flowers at least once a month

Rationale:
A) Helps you remember how nice it is to get flowers
B) Helps you remember the effort and thought required to give flowers

Investment Tip #3

Maintain Perception of Your Stock's Value: Keep your shoes looking nice

Rationale:
You may not have the kind of job or lifestyle that requires fancy shoes, but many a first impression has been made not by the clothing or the hair, but by the shoes. Shoes tell a lot about a person, like whether they are observant enough to notice that their shoes are scuffed up and covered in mud. Shoes are the windows to the soul. So whether you wear Nikes or Gucci's, keep them as looking fresh as possible. Soap and water, mink oil, shoe polish, a neighborhood cobbler (yes, that word is still in use), or a personal shopper are all resources you should consider.

Investment Tip #4

Take plenty of risks, because this is the only way rewards are earned. BUT, only risk what you can afford to lose.

Rationale:
Dive into new situations and relationships, give of yourself freely, but at the same time don't bet the farm. Many a savvy stock broker or land speculator has lost it all, including their self respect, on a sure thing. So can you.

Investment Tip #5

If You Don't Understand It, Don't Invest in It

Rationale:
An old saying in Finance is that if you don't understand it, don't invest in it. That is, even when a hundred people tell you how great an investment is and how it's a really hot tip, if you don't understand the explanation no matter how many times you hear it, don't put your time and money into it. Doing so is essentially a bet, you have no clue on the mechanisms for success or failure, you are just going

on someone else's word. A lot of people lose a ton of money because they don't listen to this advice. You should keep this in mind when dating. If you don't understand a person to the point that their thoughts and actions are alien to you, don't invest in them. This is not to say that if a person is different, or foreign, or unique, or from another way of life then you should not pursue a relationship. Many people find these differences attractive, alluring, and quite meaningful. They find common points of interest and concern, and their different-ness and uniqueness are complementary. The situation that you should avoid is the person who doesn't show up on time for no good reason, doesn't seem interested in you when they say are, doesn't act in any predictable way in situations such as meeting your friends and family, or can't explain what they do for a living. You don't understand it, don't invest in it.

Investment Tip #6

Support Positive Investments.

Rationale:
Going on a great date isn't enough. You can't just say to yourself, "that was a great use of my time, maybe I'll see them later if they call," and then you're off to take care of business without a word. If you want someone to go out with you again, you have to let them know that you had a good time. You have to let them know that you really felt that you made a good investment of your time, and would be open to future reinvestments. Tell them this at the end of the date, don't be shy. Furthermore, because good investments are hard to find, be proactive and call them later the next day to tell them again. No preening or fawning is required, just a simple, "I had a good time," or even, "Thank you." If even one of you is on your toes, you could also drop them a line later in the week to chat about a topic or situation that came up on your date, about which you just happened to be thinking or saw on television or heard on the radio. This shows that you were interested in what you heard and did together. Remember, interest is very attractive.

Investment Tip #7

Three is the Magic Number.

Rationale:
In all of your dating activities, one thing to never forget is the almost mystical nature of the number three. The third telephone call is when we begin to feel more relaxed when speaking with a person. The third date is when we often decide if a relationship is emerging. The third person that we see while simultaneously dating two others is when things start falling apart.

Trying to date two people at the same time is very common. We often ask why we should limit ourselves to just one when we could have two, especially if a relationship is not monogamous. We can handle two, we can give each person the attention they need, and in turn we get double our pleasure, double our fun. But three is an altogether different story. Three is what is known as a "deal killer." When dating three different persons we begin to lose our edge. We have less time. We have less money. We are less focused. Things become more complex. We have to begin balancing resources in favor of some people and away from others. We start to say, "Hey, I don't have to worry about them, I've two extra to spare!" At this point things start to fall apart, not just in one relationship, but in all three. It's a domino effect, as your reaction to each ping-pongs into the others. Prospect #1 - gone! Prospect #2 - gone! Prospect #3 - going, going, gone! In the end, you are left with nothing, again dateless on a Saturday night.

Investment Tip #8

Save Something for a Rainy Day.

Rationale:
In this case, we mean literally a "rainy day." Rainy days are when you and your date have done everything, tried everything, experienced everything, and are starting to get a little bored. That's when you bring out that something special you've been saving for a rainy day. Make sure it's special. Make sure they'll like it. Make sure they won't forget it.

Return on Investment (ROI)

One way to make sure that you're on track and meeting your dating goals is to perform a ROI analysis. ROI stands for Return on Investment. This is the percentage of profit that you get back from an investment, after revenue and costs have been factored in. The formula for ROI is calculated:

ROI = Return/Investment = (Revenue-Costs)/Costs

Many firms use ROI to determine if they can use their investment resources better elsewhere. They say, "I can get a 10% return just by sticking my money in the bank, so any investment needs to have an ROI greater than 10%." You can say they same thing when it comes to your love life. You can say, "I can get a 5% ROI just by going back to my ex, so any investment in someone new needs to have an ROI greater than 5%."

Of course, 5% is pretty low, don't you think?

To do a ROI analysis for romance, you need to assign values to each possible outcome as if it were revenue. Let's assume that the cost of a date in dinner, clothing, hair, gas, and breath mints is $25.00 (forget the fact that this number doesn't come from Reality as we know it). Then let's look at possible outcomes.

Each person will value the outcome differently, based on their own priorities and objectives.

Outcome	Bob's Valuation	Maria's Valuation
Kissing	20	15
Had a good time	45	30
Agreed on another date	10	35
Had Sex	40	10
Not Bored Tonight	10	20

Now let's look at the ROI for each of these situations:

Outcome	Bob's Valuation	Maria's Valuation
Kissing	(20-25)/25= -20%	(15-25)/25= -40%
Had a good time	(45-25)/25= 80%	(30-25)/25= 20%
Agreed on another date	(10-25)/25= -60%	(35-25)/25= 40%
Had Sex	(40-25)/25= 60%	(10-25)/25= -60%
Not Bored Tonight	(10-25)/25= -60%	(20-25)/25= -20%

As you can see, the ROI analysis for Bob and Maria tell them whether they should continue investing their resources after tonight's date.

Note: If Bob or Maria live in San Francisco, their ROI's may change. In a recent "Best of the Bay" edition of the popular San Francisco Bay Guardian, readers top vote for the Best First Date Activity: *Sex.*

Generating more Revenue:
Sales Promotions

Unlike traditional advertising, which creates reasons and desire to buy a product, sales promotion gives the potential customer short-term incentive to purchase. Several factors have increased the use of sales promotions, including an increase in the number of brands (especially similar ones) and a decrease in the effectiveness of basic advertising resulting from an increasingly "niche-oriented" consumer market.

Sales promotions often attract customers who are not loyal to a specific brand. They primarily look for a low price and good value. In markets where brands are very similar, sales promos can generate a short-term increase in sales, but not a lot of permanent gain in your market share.

In target markets where brands are not very much alike, sales promotions may be used to permanently change market shares.

One reason you would obviously want to use a sales promotion is when you are after short-term gains in a market with very little customer loyalty, real or perceived. Men vacationing at Hedonism II, in Jamaica, or at Club Med, Anywhere, might not exhibit a lot of loyalty to the person they met on the first night when there are so many other "brands" to try out.

Likewise, unmarried celebrities such as professional athletes may not show a huge amount of customer loyalty. They tend to have offers for test trials on a regular basis. In this situation, a common market strategy used is a promotion. The logic is that if the customer actually tries your product offering then it's very likely that they will really, really like it. In fact, they may like it so much that they toss all the other competition out of bed. We call this strategy "Wishful thinking". With little product loyalty a sales promo might get your target's short-term attention for a night or even a week, but probably will not result in a permanent gain in market share. Don't hock your car and call your folks just because you think it will. Unless you really are Mr. Universe or Ms. America, they will not be sticking around to make a commitment.

If your goal however really is a short-term increase in your product sales (for whatever reason, which we won't even go into here) then a sales promo is your perfect medium. Hopefully both of you get what you want.

I went to a party once with my girlfriends thrown by [Famous Actor/Comedian, that we will call "Sammy"] at our University. We were pretty excited, because his buddies went around campus, handing out flyers to all of the good-looking women. We got a couple of flyers, and knew we were pretty hot. So we got all-dressed up and went to the party.

When we got to his hotel suite and opened the door, the room was packed. But there were no men. Just "Sammy" and his pals and a hundred women. All these women were everywhere, dressed up, made-up, and they were posing! They were doing their best to get "Sammy's" attention.

"Sammy" was eating it up, playing the room, because he knew what time it was. What was worse was that I even caught myself trying to get his attention. It was unbelievable!

But it was a good party, despite the fact that there were no men. I heard that this one girl did stay with "Sammy" that night. I just didn't know who she was until the next day.

She didn't go to class until lunch time, then she pulled up in front of Union Hall in his limo. Everyone was there because it was lunch and classes were out, so we all saw her drive up. She got out of this stretch limo, and wanted everybody to see her. She was proud of herself. She was making a big deal out of it, stepping out of the limo with help, looking around with her sunglasses on. You know. But to top it all off, the real killer, was that she was wearing a sweatshirt from his show that had his name on it: "Sammy."

As in, "I got Sammy."

Let me tell you, people were not impressed. In fact, starting that day no one even called her by her real name anymore. They just referred to her condescendingly as "Sammy."

A very common promo is "the favor." As in, "I'll do you a favor (the promo) and you'll like me more." These are cheap shots, usually winning very short-term gains, if any. You may do favors for friends, but when you do them for dates the outcome is variable. If they liked you already then they may like you more, but if they were neutral or negative before then they'll like you for about as long as that favor takes to fade from their minds. They will show you little to no brand loyalty.

What is "a date favor"? A date favor falls in the area of: "Yeah, I can get concert tickets for the big show tomorrow night. No problem." Then you're thinking, "Yeah, they'll be impressed because I got the tickets, thankful because I paid for them, and after we have a good time they'll really want to go out with me again." They're thinking, "Great, I can see the concert." They are rarely thinking, "What a great person, now we can spend some quality time while watching a fabulous concert." It's hard to admit, but if someone else had offered tickets, your date would have gone with them in a heartbeat. Date favors are a form of self-stimulation, at best. Stay focused, be strategic, don't waste your resources.

Promotions are best used when you already have positive market share or customer awareness, and are trying to make further inroads. Our all-time favorite promo is the occasional offer to cook dinner for a date. It's a great deal for both parties. You get to lock-in a commitment for another shot at getting together, they get waited on. You get to exercise your culinary skills, they get to eat. Food prepared and served by hand is a time-tested aphrodisiac, and if you throw in some wine, music, oysters, and chocolates you probably could sell your after-dinner memoirs to cable TV.

"Occasional" is the operative word, however. When you cook regularly it becomes an expected service, not an attention getting promotional strategy. The promo loses freshness and exceeds its shelf life. [See the More Advice for Promotional Recipe ideas]

Whenever using a promo keep this advice in mind:

- Set clear goals
  (what you want to achieve)

- Stay within your budget
  (time, energy, money, food, tolerance for pain, etc.)

- Leverage partnerships
  (double-date, blind-dates, etc.)

The Economic Cycle of Dating

Dating is like the economy, you have periods of exciting growth and periods of disturbing decline (recessions). Recessions are of course the ones that we want to avoid, but as they say, "trees don't grow to the sky." Things don't go on forever, pauses happen. It's boom or bust.

These periods of declining growth affect all kinds of areas in your personal life, including productivity, consumer confidence, investment, and return on investment (ROI).

But you can be ready. Knowing that a recession is coming is not enough. To weather the cycle, you must prepare for it.

Recession Proofing Your Love Life

Start with the basics, and you can recession proof your love life as much as humanly possible. Realistically speaking, jobs, dates, and sex are all pretty hard to guarantee, especially sex (legally, at least). Still, there are some things that you can do to maximize your chances of weathering the storm.

First, recession proof your life. To do that, make sure you know who your friends are, where your family lives, and if your pets are being fed every day. Clean your place. Keep it ready for unexpected company. Wear fresh undies. Buy a cookbook and some new hot spices. Take a class. Send a letter or email to past coworkers about your job and good movies. Buy some peach ice cream. Keep hope alive.

Dress for Success. From a clothing perspective, there are two schools of thought. The first is that a recession is a somber time, and one should dress in subtle hues such as browns, blacks and grays. These come in handy for many

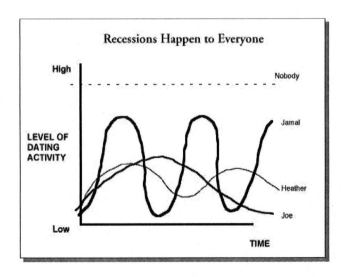

Recessions Happen to Everyone

reasons, including not ironing due to lack of inspiration, and the ability to look chic and urban even on a Kentucky horse farm.

The second school of thought is that we should bring zest and joy to our lives by wearing bright, emotion enhancing colors such as yellows, oranges, and reds. These are particularly useful if one is trying to stand out in the crowd (see, Advertising), or trying to avoid being hit crossing the street while looking at ones feet.

Either school is fine. Just try to avoid gaining more than five extra pounds during a recession. It's not strategic, it's tactical. Gaining weight is recession-proofing only if you plan on starving.

As with all countries, governments, and economies, everyone experiences recessions. E-v-e-r-y-o-n-e. But everyone experiences them differently - one person's minor recession is another's major Depression. Keep in mind, though, that with a recession the question is not "if" or "when," but rather "how long?" How long is really up to you. Like all economies, it's a matter of when you decide to start reinvesting in the future.

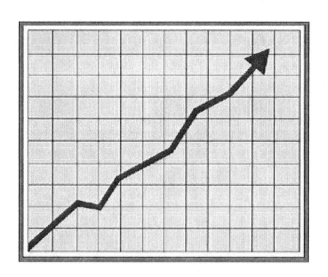

NEGOTIATIONS

"Ah me! for aught that ever I could read,
Could ever hear by tale or history,
The course of true love never did run smooth."
                          - Shakespeare, Two Gentlemen of Verona

Negotiation is a part of all relationships. We negotiate with almost everyone with which we have any meaningful contact. Cars, food, jobs, homes, salaries, gas money, sex, dinner time, we negotiate for it all on various levels. We negotiate so much that according to popular belief we actually get better over time. This couldn't be farther from the truth. We don't get better, we just get more sophisticated.

> **Grade School Negotiating Tactic**: "If you don't let me have it then I'll hate you forever! You're evil!"

> **High School Negotiating Tactic**: "If you don't let me have it then I won't be a [man/woman]. You love me, don't you? Everyone else is doing it. You know you can trust me."

> **College Negotiating Tactic**: "Why not? Don't you know we're in college now. We're not at home with our parents. We're adults. Want another drink?"

> **Grown-Up Negotiating Tactic**: "What, you don't want to? You're kidding, right? So what are we doing here? I've got things to do."

Guilt and pressure, how persuasive.

In business school it's important to learn about negotiations for two reasons. The first is so that we can become successful in business. The second is so that we don't kill each other because every student is a self-confident verbose know-it-all. Many a group meeting has turned into a free-for-all of people claiming to know the right answers because, "I did this work before b-school" or "I interned at a company with the same problem" or ,"I know this is the way to do it because that's how they do it in consulting, and I'm going into consulting." The consultants-to-be and the former attorneys are always the hardest to get to join the general consensus.

Getting To Yes

A lot of people think that the way to win a negotiation is to out-debate or out-talk the other person. In fact, we all do it from time to time. We take a position, and then we argue for it. We take a side and we get personally involved in the issue. Since we're personally involved, any criticism of our position is a criticism of us, and we react as if we've been personally attacked. From there things go downhill fast, with name calling and "Screw you!" and "You idiot" all around the table. Simple topics such as "what should we eat for dinner?" or "where should we go on vacation?" or "what movie should we see tonight?" or "why are you using that drawer?" devolve into ridiculous fights that no one understands.

Researchers Roger Fisher and William Ury, authors of the ground-breaking book, "Getting to Yes: Negotiating Agreements Without Giving In," call this "positional bargaining." That is, we take a position and fight for it on a personal level. For the reasons above, they claim this is unproductive. The results usually are win-lose, and in the end neglect both parties' interests. Better to use, they advise, "principled" negotiation as a more satisfying method for reaching mutually satisfying agreements.

Principled negotiation consists of four main principles:

• Separate the people from the problem
  (Don't see the person as the problem, see the problem as the problem.)

• Focus on interests rather than positions
  ("What are we really trying to resolve?", instead of "where do I stand on this issue?")

• Generate a variety of options before settling on an agreement
  (Force yourselves not to make a decision, a judgement, or even a critical observation until you've created a list of alternatives. Focus on shared interests.)

• Insist that the agreement be based on objective criteria
  (Agree on the criteria for your decision before you begin negotiations, or before you begin reviewing the options. Make sure the criteria are objective by seeing if both sides would abide by them under all circumstances)

When using these principles you can come to much better solutions than simply arguing for your side. But it's tough. You have to remember that if someone criticizes your ideas, they are not criticizing you personally. If they are, then say, "Hold on right there big fella'/little missy, what has that got to do with the topic?" If they say, "It's because you're always blah, blah, blah" then take the high road and say, "well, that's not the case now, so why don't you think this idea is a good option?"

Another tactic you could use is sidestepping and rephrasing the criticism. You could say, "Yeah, smart ass, what makes you think you're right?", but it's better to rephrase what they're saying in a way that sounds logical and non-critical of you, and see if they agree with your understanding of the dumb thing they just said. Try not to let them know you think it's dumb, as that would be counterproductive. When they see that you're considering their ideas and rejecting them because they aren't the best option, not because of the source of the idea, then you can more easily get them to move in the direction of the best solution.

The Best Alternative To A Negotiated Agreement

A lot of people are scared that whatever the agreement, they may get the short end of the stick. They may get stuck with a really bad deal. They may have to eat something that they really don't want anywhere near their mouths. Just remember, you want an agreement that is good for both sides, or at least is what is known as the "Best Alternative to a Negotiation Agreement", or BATNA. If your BATNA is walking away from the discussion empty-handed, that's your cutoff point for negotiations. You do not want to go below it. Your BATNA is not your "position" A position is not the Best Alternative to a Negotiation Agreement. Your position, though, may have a BATNA.

The following are a list of possible topics for negotiation, annotated with Susan's personal BATNAs:

Topic for Negotiation	Susan's Position	Susan's BATNA
When to smoke Cigars	A lady can smoke them if she feels like it, it's her mouth	Calling old buddy former President Clinton and asking him if he wants a toke
Which Movies	I hate movies with slashers chasing after young women, trying to cut them open with a butcher knife. That's not my idea of entertainment	Chasing him around his apartment with a steak knife to see how he likes it. Make him scream, "Stop Susan, stop, please Susan, you're scaring me!" Now that's entertaining
Restaurants	No more cheap diners. They're cute and cozy, but I just can't stand the grease. At least make sure it doesn't have crusty old food left on the forks	Pizza delivery to my house, with all the toppings that I want: garlic, anchovies, artichokes, olives, pepperoni, triple cheese, extra garlic, ham, and a dash of smoked duck meat. He has to eat at least half the pizza.
Cleanliness	Wash your hands buddy before you touch me. I saw you pick your nose, take a leak in the alley, and shake hands with the garbage collector during his rounds. My name is not "Typhoid Mary."	Carry a bottle of anti-bacterial soap in purse. Hand to him in front of his buddies and say, "This ought to clear up that little infection. You said it's not contagious, right?"
Who Drives	I can drive as well as he can, but since I drive every day and he doesn't, he should drive	Take a taxi, and call him a "lazy SOB" when I see him, make him pay for the fare after I have the taxi circle the block five times before dropping me off.
Vacation Spots	Nowhere south of Texas or North of Chicago	Go visit my sister by myself in Rome, call Paolo and see if he's still got that urge to learn everything there is to know about American women.
Who Pays	I'll pay for myself, unless you want to take me someone expensive, then you better be ready to pay through the nose...I don't take well to teasing	Alright, I'll let him pay for the cheap stuff too if he insists, but that doesn't mean that he's 'getting any' later

98

What's In It For Me?

Many successful business persons, those who have been around for a long-time and have built profitable enterprises, will agree that the key to successful negotiations is to figure out not only what's in it for me, but what's in it for you too. It's easy to fight for what we want and believe, but it's more effective to understand the other person's battle, and then work out a way to give them part of that. As Dale Carnegie wrote in his ground-breaking book, "How To Win Friends and Influence People:"

Try Honestly to See Things from the Other Person's Point of View

Dale says this is one of the principal means to winning them over to your way of thinking. In dating there are many times when we want people to agree with us.

> "What do you want to eat?"
> "How about Italian"
> "Pizza, pasta, or lasagna? (I really do not want pasta, I've been eating it too much lately and am getting as big as a house)"
> "Yeah, pasta sounds good."
> "Anywhere you want to go? (let's see what they have in mind)"
> "How about Big Freddies over on South Street?"
> "Oh yeah, big Freddies, that's not bad. (OK, so they may just want to go over to South Street. Let's see..). Hey, have you tried that new Chinese restaurant on South Street? They say it's pretty good. Want to try something new? (a little temptation never hurts)"
> "Is it good?"
> "That's what they say. I tell you what. Why don't we check it out? It could be really nice. If not, then next time we can go to Big Freddies. (do we have a deal?)"
> "That sounds good."
> "Cool. (deal closed)"
> "Great."

Of course, deciding on where to eat is one of the easier of dating negotiations. In fact, we could place them on the low level of the Three Levels of Importance. Level 1 are topics that you can win or lose fairly regularly, and if you don't lose too often then you don't feel bad. If you lose too often they suddenly become major cannon fodder of abuse and neglect.

Level 2 are things that you really want to win. Occasionally you may lose, but you make a point of trying to get your way eventually.

Level 3 are issues that you feel you absolutely cannot lose, at any cost.

Examples of various Dating issues, and their corresponding levels for Amanda:

Level 1

- Japanese food, yes
- Ethiopian food, yes
- "Friends" has been one of the funniest sitcoms on TV
- Saturday Night Live is no longer funny unless they're making fun of the President
- This is my favorite T-shirt
- I prefer to go to the movies or a show on first dates
- Hold open doors for me if you want, I won't complain
- I can eat a ton of pizza
- It's OK if my date wants to see a Sylvester Stallone movie

Level 2

- Don't ask to drive my car
- Kung-fu movies and anime are a lot of fun
- I like to read books
- I don't like the smell of cigars
- Your friend George is kind of a dufus
- These are my favorite jeans
- I prefer to go to nice restaurants on 2nd and 3rd dates
- Opening my car door for me is a little sexist
- Don't ask me to not eat fish

Level 3

- My date has to have a job
- Don't wear fur
- Don't put cream in my sauce (it makes me sick)
- Meeting at Starbucks a couple of times a week is not my idea of dating
- I smoke cigarettes
- These are my favorite shoes
- SUV's are harmful to the environment
- I prefer to do something socially conscious together after a month or two of dating
- Don't ever ask me for money
- Veal is cruel
- The Detroit Pistons suck

If you go by Dale Carnegie's advice, it is especially important when you get to Level 2 and 3 to figure out what the other person wants. You have to know what Level the issue represents for them. If you're Level 3 and they're Level 3, someone is going to win big, and someone is going to lose big, and the loser may not like it in the least.

Avoiding the topic is one dating negotiation strategy. Feign illness, loss of hearing, preoccupation with your salad, compliment their choice in shoes, or launch into an entirely different conversation. You could avoid Level 3 issues as much as possible until you are well-established in a relationship. Then you can cut lose the cannons. This strategy is the direction in which many people head, and we actually recommend it for one basic reason: "Zero percent of zero is zero". In other words, as once put in a famous R&B song, "Nothin' from nothin' leaves nothin." You can win big, and have nothing of value to show for it.

What if Level 3 is a serious personal value issue for at least one of you, like Save the Whales, or Writer's Rights, or Recycling? Sometimes Level 3 takes on a religious-like state of seriousness. In this case, maybe you might want to know about it up front so that you can decide if a relationship even has a chance. That is logical and well thought out. When doing business this is often the way to go. Why waste time establishing a partnership when the two firms will not be able to agree on core directional issues, such as whether to worship or vilify Microsoft. The business-school advise is to "know all the issues" beforehand. Not knowing the issues, including cultural and organizational ones, is why a large number of strategic partnerships, mergers, and acquisitions fail.

On the other hand, you can live with a lot of conflicting issues if you really care about a person. That is, if they have value to you; if the ROI passes the return threshold.

So what should you do to be a better negotiator? Our advice is to remember the business principles above, and learn more about your opponent. Perform further customer research. Go out on a few more dates.

Don't Make a Deal that You Can't Live With

Don't go lower than your BATNA. It sounds pretty basic, but sometimes we attempt to outsmart the other person by making an offer that combines both generosity and reasonableness. Perhaps we are trying buy goodwill, or honesty, or to establish an environment of trust. These are all laudable objectives. But they are not good reasons for negotiating a deal that has your loss as its starting point. The following is a good example:

> When I lived in France as an exchange student, I had a great French
> girlfriend. She was a good catch, and after about a month of dating
> she told me that she was very cool, and if I wanted to see other
> women she was OK with it, as long as I told her about them.
>
> A few months later she found out that I was seeing a couple of
> other girls in town, and stormed into my apartment. In front of my

roommates she started crying on the floor and calling me a bloody liar.

"Liar, liar, liar," she said.

"What did I lie about?" I asked. "You said I could see other women."

"Yes I did," she replied, "but I told you to tell me about them first."

Now I ask you, what was the difference? She made the offer, and I took it. I didn't agree to her terms completely, but she was the one who offered them, not me. The way I looked at it, even if I had said, "No thanks," I still had the green light to see other women.

His girlfriend had taken a negotiating position equivalent to telling the other party that if she didn't close the deal then she would go out of business. That was her BATNA. There was nowhere to go but down.

Don't Go for Broke

You've probably heard of billionaire mogul Donald Trump's famous business novel, "The Art of the Deal," which focuses on "The Don's" fantastic skill at negotiation and high finance. A lot of people were inspired by this memoir, but after business school we were not part of that group. There's no genius here, no great manifest destiny to be a winner all the time. It all comes down to risk and reward. "High finance" doesn't require a lot of complexity or intelligence, just a willingness to risk losing a large quantity of money without the involvement of drugs. The deal part comes in reducing the risk as much as possible.

In the movie "Wall Street" they said that "Greed is Good." In the dating world greed is good, but only if you don't mind ending up with a lot of nothing of value. Greed is indeed a motivating factor. Getting everything you can is part of the free market system, but dating and relationships resemble mergers more than acquisitions. The winner-takes-all scenario is fantastic for one night stands, but not much more.

As you know, the best deal is where both parties have a chance of winning simultaneously.

I had a deal with my girlfriend that I would stop smoking if she switched from white wine to red wine. I drank red wine, and she preferred white, but it wasn't fun when she couldn't share in a good bottle. It felt like we were apart, and it wasn't a lot of fun.

Of course she told me how she didn't like the smell of cigarettes, how they were bad for me, you know the routine.

So we made a deal. She would start drinking red wine, and I would stop smoking.

It took about a year for me to stop smoking, and I feel healthier, but it was two before she drank red wine.

But now she won't drink white wine anymore.

The Customer is Always Right

Possibly true in some lines of work, but if it were universally true there would be no operating businesses left in America. Customers do not know what they are talking about half the time, and half of that half they are simply trying to get something for free, or for you to pick up the cost of their own mistakes. Granted, that leaves another 50% of the time when they actually are right, and you'd damn well better make sure that you take care of their problem, pronto.

Still, we're talking about a fifty-fifty chance. To narrow the odds of your losing something in the deal, we've come up with a more accurate statement:

"Let the Customer Think They're Right"

This is especially true in dating, where the phrase "I told you so" is an invitation for an early withdrawal.

We admit that it's hard to say when we are wrong. It's easier to tell someone else that they are. In fact, some professions don't allow you to do anything but tell other people that they are wrong. Lawyers are a good example. If this were a book written by lawyers, this chapter might be along the lines of:

> *"The Customer is Always Wrong, and I can Prove It. Unless of course they are My Client, then Everyone is Wrong except the Customer."*

Be creative. Try to find some areas in which your customer is right, even if you have to be as transparent as "your lasagna is incredible." A compliment is a form of saying that a person did at least one thing right.

Be A Hero

Sounds simple - "be a hero". We know that being a hero rocks. It sends you straight to the top of the CA charts. Save a kitten, save a corporation, save a relationship and you may find yourself on Easy Street. Just remember, one man's hero is another man's villain. When you want to play the hero, make sure you know whose side your customer is on.

Some men have friends who consider it quite heroic to meet four women a night, try to score with all of them, and then blow them off like yesterday's garbage. If that's who you want to impress with acts of heroism, go for it. You're laying the groundwork for a lot of delicate product repositioning in the future, when you try to convince the date of your dreams that you really are a nice guy. "It's just bad press, I tell you. Ancient history."

Know your target market, and be a hero there. Your pals can go see a movie.

Crisis Management

Dates basically have two outcomes. They either go as expected, or they don't. Sometimes chocolates work, sometimes they cause a rash. Sometimes your car gets you to the game on time, sometimes you get a flat tire on the way.

These outcomes, or crises, don't matter as much as how you handle them. Well-handled crises can make you stronger and more experienced. They should not shut you down. Poorly handled crises definitely will.

> My date and I were on the way to the Opera, where we were meeting friends for a big gala, when suddenly the car in front of us on the highway swerved out of the lane. We tried to figure out why, until we saw right ahead of us a mattress sitting right in the middle of the road. We were going too fast to stop, and couldn't switch lanes, so my date decided to drive over the mattress. Unfortunately, rather going over the mattress we ended up on top of the mattress, and the car skidded to a stop on the highway.

> We had been going about 60 MPH, so I figured that the car behind us would just ram us in the rear end, but amazingly it stopped in time. But when I turned around to look at it, suddenly I saw it jerk forward one, two, three, four times. My date was like, "No f---ing way!"

> When we got out of the car and walked around to see if there was any damage, we didn't have a scratch. But the car behind us was the first in a five-car pileup, and behind that was another three-car pileup.

> What was great was that my date didn't panic at all. The cops came pretty quickly, and a tow truck lifted us off of the mattress, saying how lucky were that it hadn't caught on fire, as he had often seen with cars stuck on mattresses.

> Then we just jumped in the car, went to the Opera and had a good time, with a great story to tell everyone when we got there.

> We've been together ever since.

The best advice in a crisis is to maintain composure. Try to keep a level head. If appropriate try to find the humor in a situation.

> I was dating these two women from opposite sides of town, and they both thought they were the only one. I met them about the same time, and saw no reason not to see both of them. We went out for about six months, so they were thinking that everything was serious. I guess it was, at least I acted like it. I was playing it pretty cool, and having a ball.

> One day I went over Tish's house for dinner. She said that she was making sushi, so I picked up a bottle of wine and a six-pack. Put on a clean shirt and headed over. When I got there we talked a little bit, drank some wine, and sat on the couch and started making out. At some point she got up and latched the front door, and came back and sat on the couch.

> Then Regina walked out of the bedroom. I thought I was going to pass out. They both were like, "Busted!"

> For two hours they kept me in that locked house, telling me how I wasn't as smart as I thought I was, how I was a dog, how I hurt them, how I was getting what I deserved.

> It was like a nightmare.

> The funny thing, the thing that made it actually kind of humorous, was that they looked like they really were enjoying themselves.

The Principal Rule to Successful Crisis Management: Admit when you're wrong as soon as you realize there are no alternatives. The longer you wait, the more you fight, the bigger it's going to hurt when you finally have to fess up.

Sometimes you have to tell everyone that you're at fault, as in the Tylenol poisonings of the early '80's ("We didn't make the bottles secure enough to resist tampering"), or the Exxon Valdez oil spill ("Yes, the captain was drunk"), or the third Batman movie ("George Clooney as Batman, what were we smoking?"), or when you're having an affair with your bestfriend's Ex ("That was f---ing stupid").

Sometimes you don't have to tell a lot of people that you are wrong. When you find out there's a problem, you tell those directly affected, compensate them, correct the damage, and clean up the mess.

Simple, and straightforward, that's the way to be. There's no shame in being wrong. It happens all the time. (Do you have any idea how many food recalls take place in the U.S. during a single month? They're not because the price tags are crooked.)

There are other types of crisis. These are less a question of wrong or right, and more a question of not having your plans blow up in your face. You have to close a deal within seconds or the whole thing is off. You have to end a relationship in the most graceful way possible, or look like a monster. You have to stop someone from putting their foot in their mouth. You have to watch your date puke. Below are two examples of what we mean:

Crisis Management Scenario #1

I was seeing pretty regularly this friend of my roommates, who I had met at a party at our house. You know, we had a party, we were both in the house, we liked each other, my bedroom was already there... That was a great first date. And, we kept seeing each other for about two months.

I found out during that time that she had a boyfriend who was living in another city. He wasn't really a full-time boyfriend, but they still had something going. I was cool with it, at least I thought I was. We were just hanging out, having sex a lot. But I guess I did see a boyfriend/girlfriend opportunity there. All our mutual friends thought so too.

One fine day we were at the bar with the whole gang of friends, doing tequila shots. She kept slamming down, one after the other, and we were like, "Whoa, you are the man!"

Everybody was having a good time, getting pretty wasted. Then out of the blue, bam, she starts talking about this other guy and how she misses him. I'm cool with that, but you know, it's a little embarrassing when you're kind of 'out on a date' with someone around your friends, and your date starts talking about someone else.

So I'm like, "uh, it's cool", and she's like, "blah, blah, blah (burp), I miss him, blah, blah, he's my one true love (burp)."

What am I supposed to do?

Then, when things couldn't have been worse, she pukes.

"Bla-a-a-eckkkk!"

She's covered in chunks, and she's leaning her head over the table and her hair is falling all into it. Stuff is dripping down her face, up her nose, and still everyone's looking at me like, "She's your girlfriend, aren't you going to help her?"

Crisis Management Scenario #2

I had been dating this girl for about a month, and things were going pretty good. We liked each other, you could tell, but we hadn't really crossed over completely into the relationship having truly romantic implications. You know, one or two kisses. Sometimes on the lips, sometimes on the cheek. It could go either way.

I needed to plant a flag in the ground and say, "hey, I'm interested in romantic, not platonic." So Valentine's Day was coming up, and I figured this was the perfect opportunity. I offered to make her dinner, my special dinner, with ginger prawns and curry chicken, a bottle of wine, and a little jazz in the background. She said let's do it, and the date was set.

On Valentine's Day I was at home making the food that I would take over her house, when a freak winter blizzard started up. It was bad, and falling hard. We talked on the phone and she said that we could do it another time, but I knew that this was a make it or break it time for our relationship. So I said, "No, no. It's not the bad out. I'll take the subway over and see you in an hour."

Dinner went pretty well. We ate, we hung out, we joked around and had a good time. But as it got late, the snow outside piled up. I mean, it was like six feet of snow drifts out there, and rising. My date said that it was too bad out for me to go home on public transportation, and she generously offered to let me sleep over.

Alright, he scores!!!

Then she said, "On the couch."

Well, I was not going to cross backwards into the platonic area of guy friend. The couch would have set that tone forever. So you know what I did? Let's just say that it was a very cold, very long walk back home that night.

This man knew his Best Alternative To A Negotiated Agreement, and he followed it all the way home during a blizzard. When the time is right, so will you.

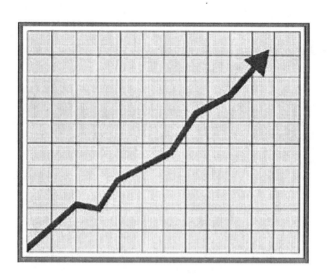

CONSULTING

"He that won't be counselled can't be helped"
- Benjamin Franklin

"Never tell people how to do things. Tell them what
to do and they will surprise you with their ingenuity."
- George S. Patton, Jr.

Sometimes your own efforts and strategies are not enough. When this happens, it's time for you to turn to a consultant.

Consulting is the profession in which people turn to someone else to define, identify, and recommend possible ways to solve a problem. Consultants are very useful, as they can fill in gaps of experience and knowledge that you may not have. They can also provide other attributes that you may currently lack. Consultants can be the following, even when you aren't:

- Objective
- Observant
- Critical
- Forward Thinking
- Pragmatic
- Helpful
- Able to bring a fresh perspective on the situation

On the other hand, they have their unique problems. They can be:

- Arrogant
- Impractical
- Expensive
- Extravagant
- Intrusive
- Annoying
- Self-Serving
- Hard to get rid of

Once you open the door to consultants they keep coming back to offer more assistance. They are a veritable Pandora's Box of advice. When working with consultants you need to know that you're wielding a double-edged sword. Still, the Pros of using consultants often outweigh the Cons. More often than not their advice is closer to accurate than your own counsel.

Potential Consultants

The list of who can be a useful consultant is quite long. It includes Friends, Family, the Ex (all of them), Potential Dates, People that You've Secretly Lusted After, Therapists, Clergy, Television Talk Shows, even [gasp] Siblings. Many people like the impersonal touch, however, and turn to mass media consultants such as Dear Abby, Dear Anne, and Horoscopes.

Horoscopes are the most innovative form of consulting. Whether you believe or not in the ability to tell your fortune based on the alignment of stars and planets into imagined constellations created by bored people looking to the sky before the days of cheap airfares and television, one thing is true about horoscopes: Essentially, they give good advice.

"Don't stick your head in the fire." Good advice. "Be nice to your boss today." Good advice. "Try to be empathetic to your lover, and don't be a pig." Good advice.

Examples of Horoscopic Advice

•Aries: Venus is in your House. Come on out and play. Eat something you like. Tonight listen to good music.

•Taurus: Get out of bed without worrying about today, let it take you where it will. Call your friends. Money is important, but not as important as you think it is. Do what you think is going to take you to the goal posts. You won't regret it.

•Sagittarius: Dancing with Devil under the pale moon light is how you feel, but don't give in. The Devil you know is not better than the Devil you don't. Your enemies have a snowball's chance in hell of convincing the world that you are wrong. The Devil take them. But remember, the Devil is in the details.

Beware

Beware people who give you advice but aren't looking after your best interests. There are a lot of them out there. Often, they are just looking for another source of entertainment, as you shoot yourself in the foot while putting it in your mouth.

How can you know the difference between good advice and bad advice? The easiest way is to try it out and see what happens. The obvious problem is that you might get slapped in the face, punched in the mouth, sued for harassment, and thrown out of your house. Most of us wouldn't like that. So instead, we recommend that you listen to the advice, ask the person what they would do if it were them, and what exactly will occur. After they drone on unconvincingly, ask them why they think that they are right. What experience have they had that says this will work? Be skeptical. Check their facts.

Don't get us wrong, if someone advises you that the person standing near the front counter has been checking you out, and that you should casually saunter over and ask that person if they know whether any good food is served at the bar, we recommend that you take this advice immediately. If this consultant has given enough thought to the details that they are providing introductory points of conversation, then they've given it enough thought to know that you will come back and bop them in the head if it's a joke.

Consulting Analysis: Is This Date a Star or a Dog?

Sometimes you have to look at a relationship and know when to stick with it, and when to pull the plug. It's not an easy decision for most people, but fortunately the Boston Consulting Group has made it easy for us. Back in 1973 they created the BCG Growth Matrix, and used it to review a company's overall portfolio of businesses and products. The Matrix is designed to use performance metrics such as cash flow to determine business strategy and investments; essentially, what to keep and what to discard.

The way the Matrix works is you assign performance metrics to each project, and then review how the projects perform against them. Cash flow and market share or growth are often used as standard performance metrics. For example, projects can have high cash flow/high market share, high cash flow/low market share, low cash flow/high market share, and low cash flow/low market share. They are then labeled a Star, a Question Mark, a Cash Cow, or a Dog depending on where they fall on the Matrix.

Stars

Stars are major contributors to revenue with strong competitive positions. You want to continue to invest in them so that they grow and reach their full potential. If you have a person that you think is a Star, you should put as much time into them as possible to maximize the possibility of positive long-term results.

Question Marks

Question Marks have low market share and fast growth, but you don't know if they have what it takes. Since they're usually early stage relationships you need to put a fairly significant amount of investment into them to grow their market share or cash flow. You think they have Star potential, so you'll put into it what will push them into that category. A lot of early romantic relationships fall into the Question Mark area, often without merit. Think about it. Do you really think that this person has the potential to be a Star, or are you just grasping at straws?

Cash Cows

Cash cows generate revenue and cash flow greater than the amount of investment required to maintain them. A lot of men and a fair amount of women seem to think that this is the ideal situation. Minimum investment, maximum return. One phone call = get sex. Dinner and a movie = get sex. Saying, "I really like you" = get sex.

Maybe it is ideal, since they tend to be later-stage relationships where large upfront investments to foster growth and market share have already been made. At this point you are basically just reaping the rewards.

Cash cows are the most desired situations, especially in business, since they can maintain an entire company with their revenue stream, as well as fuel growth and investment in new enterprises that are Stars and Questions Marks, the Cash Cows of the future.

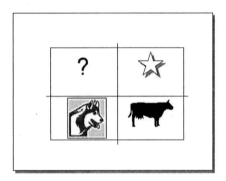

Dogs

Dogs are dogs. (On the other hand, not all men are dogs) Dogs are under-performing businesses. Even though they contribute some minor cash flow, they are eventually destined for the trash heap as they are either harvested for all they're worth, or divested and shopped off to someone else who thinks they're a potential Star or Cash Cow. In dating, don't waste your time on Dogs, even if that's all you have. Dogs are dogs, and rarely will large amounts of investment turn them around. The other side of the coin is that in certain competitive situations dogs may have some value as part of your overall portfolio. They can perhaps help your negotiating position. Or they may simply reduce the pressure